Confrontation And Intervention In The Modern World

By

URS SCHWARZ

1970

OCEANA PUBLICATIONS, INC.

DOBBS FERRY, NEW YORK.

Library of Congress Catalog Card Number: 78-102940

International Standard Book Number: 0-379-00380-5

MANUFACTURED IN THE UNITED STATES OF AMERICA

Table of Contents

iii

Foreword

To Americans today, "confrontation" and "intervention" are supercharged with electric tension generated by the Cuban missile crisis of 1962, the civil war in the Dominican Republic in 1965, tht prolonged involvement in Vietnam, and the portent of the Middle East. Acute as are our sensibilities to both practices, our sense of their evolution and contemporary meaning remains blurred.

In this penetrating volume, Urs Schwarz examines intervention and confrontation as doctrine and as practice, in historical perspective but with a contemporary focus. He analyzes them with rigor and a cool objectivity containing no trace of cold detachment. A thoroughgoing European, he has long felt at home in America during his frequent visits here. For a quarter of a century the Foreign Editor of the *Neue Zürcher Zeitung* and for more than a decade the editor of the English-language *Swiss Review of World Affairs,* also published in Zurich, he took a leave of absence in 1965 to undertake a comprehensive inquiry into the development of strategic thought in the United States. Now retired from his formal editorial responsibilities, he devotes his working hours to reflection and commentary on the politico-military thought and behavior of modern states.

Urs Schwarz treats "confrontation" as an exercise in mutual deterrence, a means of limiting the use of force and pursuing objectives without resort to war. He identifies twenty-three such confrontations in the period since World War II, commencing with the Berlin blockade of 1948-49 and extending to the border incidents between Communist China and the Soviet Union in 1969. In his roster, only six of the twenty-three confrontations directly involved the United States of America and the Soviet Union; in seventeen, some shooting occurred; and in a few the level of violence rose to a point barely short of full-scale war. As a strategy to limit the use of armed force in the pursuit of national goals, confrontation plainly leaves much to be desired.

In Mr. Schwarz's usage, "intervention," like "confrontation," is conceived as a strategy to limit the use of armed force and to keep events under the control of the actor in its pursuit of its national goals. It involves an act by a powerful state in relation to one much weaker; it is intended by the intervenor to vindicate a rule or principle or pattern of politics, morality, or law; it is aimed at the structure of political authority in the target society which it seeks either to change or to protect against a change imposed by others; it represents a sharp break with the preexisting attitudes and behavior of the intervenor; and it is limited in character, scale, and time.

In the practice of the United States and of the Soviet Union since World War II, principles or patterns of politics, morality, or law which the intervenor sought to vindicate have constituted an identifying thread of continuity running through the varied incidents.

The Soviet Union has typically intervened to support its doctrine of "wars of national liberation" or its Brezhniev doctrine, according to which it is declared to be the duty of the Soviet Union to intervene in behalf of the "world socialist community" into any socialist state which has been frightened or seduced by counter-revolution into a betrayal of its own allegedly true interests as a part of world socialism.

For the United States, Urs Schwarz traces the pattern of intervention along lines marked by the Truman doctrine, the Eisenhower doctrine, and subsequent comparable enunciations by President Kennedy and President Johnson down to the break represented by the Nixon doctrine. In his State of the Union Message to Congress on January 22, 1970, President Nixon explained the basis of a doctrine which he had first announced at Guam on July 28, 1969:

> "Neither the defense nor the development of other nations can be exclusively or primarily an American undertaking. The nations of each part of the world should assume the primary responsibility for their own well-being; and they themselves should determine the terms of that well-being.
>
> "We shall be faithful to our treaty commitments, but we shall reduce our involvement and our presence in other nations' affairs."

Mr. Schwarz stresses the potential implications of the Nixon doctrine as a new departure in U.S. policy, but he reminds us that more is required than statements in Washington to realize the potentialities. The outcome will depend on the "feasibility of a policy of restraint and aloofness in the modern international environment. And it depends on how long the Soviet Union will adhere to its preposterous Brezhniev doctrine . . ." It will also depend on the specific applications of the general Nixon doctrine and on the re-establishment of mutual understanding among the Presidency, the Congress, and the American People.

Milton Katz

Cambridge, Massachusetts
August 12, 1970

Chapter I

The Need Of Limiting Conflict

Moral and Strategic Factors

Throughout the centuries human conflict was naturally limited. The limiting factors were the smallness of organized political bodies—families, tribes, groups under feudal suzerainty, cities—the loose character of most alliances, the short range of weapons, the lack of communications, the slow motion of armed forces. Besides, the instinct of self-preservation as expressed and formulated in traditional rules of warfare, often clad in religious forms, codes of chivalry, codes of diplomatic and political behavior, was a living force. Some of the limitations prevented the full use of one's military capabilities; some were the result of limited military capability, which, then, was used to the full, within these limits. It was the nineteenth century with its growth of centralized authority and its technological revolutions which removed all voluntarily accepted or self-imposed limits. The Napoleonic wars and the Italian wars marked the transition in Europe. The new concept triumphed for the first time in the American Civil War of 1861 to 1865. The colonial wars of the late eighteenth and the nineteenth centuries, in which moral limitations did not apply vis-a-vis the "uncivilized" peoples to be brought under European (including Russian) or American domination, may have been another element favoring the transition to "total war." This implied that the only limits were those of the actual military capabilities, which were then used to the full.

Everything has been said about "total war," the unlimited character of warfare in the two world crises of 1914-19 and 1939-45. Out of the ashes of this devastating conflict familiar

1

patterns seemed to emerge again: The colossal technological change introduced by the invention of nuclear and thermo-nuclear weapons and intercontinental delivery systems, accompanied by the revolution of the world system brought about by the age of decolonialization, revived the very old concept that conflict has to be voluntarily limited. It gained a dominant position. The instinct of self-preservation, after its eclipse in the first half of the twentieth century, seems to have become an active force again, urging governments and peoples to adopt a more rational behavior. The fast expanding science of strategy has chosen as its main object the problem of avoiding, or at least limiting, conflict.

The development of new concepts of public international law has significantly contributed to the tendency to limit conflict. Yet, it is not only the evolution of the law of nations from the pre-World War I concept, through the intermediate stage of the collective security system of the League of Nations to the conceptual framework of the United Nations, where war is excluded as an instrument of international politics, which has brought about the deep change we are witnessing. However important legal considerations may be in the decision-making process of governments, the deepest impulses come from the political, social, strategic, economic and technological factors. In this respect, the overriding fact in our contemporary world certainly is the rise of two world powers, each representing a concentration of force, a capability for destruction, new in kind and in dimension, in the hands of one government. These two powers have used technology as a ladder, economic ambition as a motor and ideology as a guideline to create—since they are divided by opposing concepts of world order—a situation of conflict loosely referred to as the Cold War.

This contest of forces between two powers, which in their political outlook are diametrically opposed, is basically unwelcome to the world and harmful to the main antagonists. Therefore, they feel strongly impelled to try to reduce their antagonism, or at least the level on which it is expressed. Whatever may be the outcome of these attempts at lessening the tensions, at detente, finally the fact remains that for the time being their relationship is placed in the shadow of their mutual power to destroy one another.

This extraordinary and catastrophic possibility, such as rarely has existed in history between antagonists, and never to the extent we witness today, becomes the source of the equally extraordinary power equilibrium which has dominated the world scene for almost a score of years and which has shaped it in many different directions. The main result is that the world powers try to avoid becoming engaged in an open conflict which might escalate into thermonuclear war. Lesser nations, on the other hand, have gained some freedom of maneuver, since the world powers prevent each other, to a large degree, from taking action against unruly and too active small members of the family of nations. This freedom of maneuver, though, is often limited when it might lead to a decisive war, and when the world powers fear that an inflammation of such a conflict might lead to a direct confrontation between them.

Political experience and the results of strategic research conducted in recent years lead to the conclusion that the strategic equilibrium is not really stable. As long as technological innovation in the field of armaments continues at the present pace and as long as the world powers have not renounced their efforts to overtake each other by way of technological breakthroughs, it is a delicate balance indeed. As long as the powers, paradoxically, seek security and stability by putting stability in jeopardy, the equilibrium cannot be considered as a secure guarantee of peace. The risk of escalation of small conflict where forces get out of control, therefore, looms heavily over the international scene.

The risk certainly has been exaggerated by the primitive view that any hostile contact between forces of the two super powers would almost automatically develop into a general, and therefore thermonuclear, war. Such views are still held and expressed by Soviet analysts who seem to reflect official theory. The same view prevailed in wide circles, and even in the innermost circles of the Western decision-makers, which were infected by the irrational fears of the public during the Cuban missile crisis. This view obviously is not sound. The interest in avoiding nuclear holocaust is such that one may safely assume that the responsible leaders, fully aware, and more than aware of the danger and their terrible responsibility, would try to stop the spiral of escalation well in advance of an irreversible decision.

This danger, though, more for its extreme gravity than for its likelihood of materialization, has made a deep impact. Thus, much more than the evolution of the concepts of public international law, in many respects merely exercises in semantics when the use of the word "war" is excluded from the vocabulary of the jurist and the politician, the strategic factor has operated the deep change in the sense that war is to be avoided at almost any cost.

New Laws of War and Peace

The changes in the legal aspect, however, must not be neglected. Parallel to the sociological and political development runs a deep change in the traditional concepts of international public law. The clear distinction between peace and war, between declared war and other forms of conflict among nations, has a marked tendency to become obsolescent.

It is significant that after the end of World War II not one single conflict has been started by a declaration of war in the legal sense. In a recent study of conflict in the twentieth century[1] eighty wars and smaller armed conflicts are listed in the short period alone between the first Vietnam war of 1945 and the Nigerian civil war which broke out on July 7, 1967.

The Secretary of Defense of the United States, Robert McNamara, in a speech in Montreal in 1966 referred to 164 internationally significant outbreaks of violence between 1958 and 1966, of which fifteen were military conflicts between two or more states. In only two of these cases was a state of war recognized to exist within the meaning of international law, namely in the conflict between the Arab States and Israel, and in the war of 1965 between India and Pakistan.[2] Since 1948, when after the

---

[1] David Wood, *Conflict in the Twentieth Century*, Adelphi Paper No. 48 (London: Institute for Strategic Studies, 1968).

[2] Dietrich Schindler, "Aspects contemporains de la neutralité," *Academie de droit international, Recueil des cours*, II, 1967 (Leyden, 1967), 283.

establishment of the State of Israel hostilities broke out between the new state and its Arab neighbors, hostilities, precariously interrupted by the truces of 1949, 1956 and 1967, the Arab governments insisted that a state of war existed between the opposing nations. In 1965 Pakistan asserted for legal purposes that it was in a state of war with India, despite the fact that no declaration of war had been issued.

The legal foundation of the new international law concept is The General Treaty for the Renunciation of War as an Instrument of National Policy (Kellogg-Briand Pact) of August 27, 1928, which provided that the governments signing the treaty declare in the names of their peoples that they "condemn recourse to war for the solution of international controversies, and renounce it as an instrument of national policy in their relations with one another." This treaty has never been denounced. On the contrary, its basic concept re-emerged in the Charter of the United Nations signed on June 26, 1945, where the word "war" appears only twice, in the first line of the preamble, declaring the determination of the contracting parties "to save succeeding generations from the scourge of war", and again at the end in the transitional article 107. Otherwise the Charter refers to the "threat of force" or "use of force," "threat to the peace, breach of the peace or act of aggression," when dealing with nations infringing the principles of the organization. With reference to the enforcement of the Security Council's decision in defense of the international order, the Charter mentions "action by air, sea, or land forces" and "operations by air, sea, or land forces," "military measures," "application of armed force." In Article 51 on self-defense the term "armed attack" is used and in Article 107, referring to the enemies in World War II, the word "action" is used.

This terminology contrasts sharply with the Covenant of the League of Nations signed in Versailles on June 28, 1919. There, the signatories recognized the obligation not to resort to war. However, this obligation was made conditional on the success of the peacekeeping procedure of the League as set out in Articles 11 to 16 of the Covenant. The members agreed not to go to war until three months after the award by the arbitrators, or the judicial decision, or the report by the Council. When a nation resorts to war, it will be deemed an act of war against all other members of the League, which of course means that they may consider themselves as being legally at war with the breaker of the peace.

The League system obviously was contradictory in its terms. Yet, the basic idea was that after exhaustion of all instrumentalities of peacekeeping, war may be declared on a non-law-abiding nation only in the name of collective security.

Stability and Fluidity

The result of the complex factors involved is that the international scene has become more stable and more fluid at the same time—more stable in so far as it becomes extremely difficult to change the *status quo,* which, historically speaking, has been open to peaceful innovation only in rare cases. If open use of force must be avoided, the chances for bringing about a change becomes very slim indeed. The resulting difficulty in altering the *status quo* may even prevent the settlement and elimination of small, local conflicts. As Robert S. Osgood points out:

> Paradoxically, though, a major reason for the persistence of such conflicts is that one or sometimes both of the superpowers, anxious that their involvements in local conflicts should not lead to direct confrontations with each other, try to prevent them from resulting in wars (or at least in decisive wars)—which are historically a primary means of settling such conflicts.[3]

Fluidity, on the other hand, has been introduced by the compulsion to use more subtle, less overt means. Among them the political, material and military support of subversive or insurgent activities within the borders of another state have become an almost permanent feature. For this purpose, they are called "wars of national liberation" when in sympathy with the leading Communist powers and accordingly supported by them, or "indirect aggression" when in opposition or at least not sub-

---

[3] Thomas W. Adams and Alvin J. Cottrell, *Cyprus Between East and West,* Robert E. Osgood in the Foreword, (Baltimore: Washington Center of Foreign Policy Research, 1968), vii.

servient to Communism. The ultimate motivation is much more often of a purely local and national character than oversimplification—"communism v. capitalism," or "Muscovite imperialism v. self-determination"—would have it. Whatever the pattern of motivation, threat of force or use of force is tolerated within the family of nations to an extraordinary degree, as long as it does not involve directly the world powers. As Carl Jaspers puts it:

> Motivation and political will are such as always, but they are kept under pressure at the same time. Therefore, the world enters frequently upon situations which in earlier times would immediately have lead to war, whereas today threats, humiliation, intimidation are being tolerated to a degree unknown before.[4]

Fluidity, moreover, implies that such limited uses of force may well reverse a trend. As Albert and Roberta Wohlstetter point out in a study of the Cuban missile crisis of 1962, it is not necessarily true "that the threat of force or the use of a low level of violence. . . leads naturally to higher levels of violence."[5] As they prove, the opposite may be true; violence may be downgraded so that finally an accommodation may be achieved.

When indirect aggression does not operate as planned, and armed conflict cannot be avoided, the conflict must not be called "war." And it must be limited, from its earliest stages throughout its development, lest it degenerate or escalate to unwanted and dreaded proportions. Thus, the art of limiting conflict has become the object of extensive research; it is exercised almost daily by political leaders throughout the world. Armed forces have been re-structured with the view to being able to engage in limited operations, so as to prevent the dangers of escalation. This is true for the Western powers as well as for the leading Communist powers, despite the fact that Communist theory is very reluctant in admitting the probability of keeping a conflict limited.

The conclusion often drawn from this novel situation is that force in international relations has lost its usefulness. Such a conclusion goes way beyond realities. War as an institution

---

[4] Carl Japers, *Die Atombombe und die Zukunft des Menschen, Politisches Bewusstsein in unserer Zeit* (München, 1962), 102.

[5] Albert and Roberta Wohlstetter, *Controlling the Risks in Cuba,* Adelphi Paper No. 17 (London, 1965), 15.

may be proscribed by international law and eliminated from the vocabulary. War may be unlikely to occur between world powers because of its destructiveness and its suicidal potentialities. War may be unlikely between great powers and small nations because of the inherent dangers of escalation. War may even gradually lose its primitive appeal as humanity becomes more aware of common bonds; and human beings may be more inclined to enjoy the fruits modern technology offers them, instead of using its destructive potentialities. Yet, as Mars veils its familiar face, hundreds of smaller and lesser martial gods are unveiled.

Force has remained, so far, the only instrument for effecting changes in the international environment. Force is the last resort of a nation bent on defending its interests and rights against a hostile neighbor.[6] Force has become, as well, for reasons yet to be explored, one of the main instruments of domestic change, with all the possibilities inherent in such change for influencing the international scene. The outbreaks of domestic, especially juvenile violence, even in well organized societies considered as basically stable, such as the United States, Japan, the Federal Republic of Germany, France, the United Kingdom, are not unconnected with the overall strategic development. War in its former legalized, official form—*ultima ratio regis*—has been successfully prevented from breaking out for more than a score of years. It has been replaced, as we know only too well, by a shocking variety of procedures short of war, designed to impose the will of one government or one party or faction or group on another. These procedures are widely reported and described in detail by the mass media. The instruments for all types of subterranean war have been profusely scattered, beginning with the arming of resistance movements of World War II and continuing throughout the years at an increasing pace, in the developed and the developing world. It cannot be surprising, therefore, that the thought and the capability of using force, instead of persuasion and other forms of political action, is close at hand, whenever pressures and anxieties mount on the domestic scene.

---

[6] Robert E. Osgood and Robert W. Tucker, *Force, Order and Justice* (Baltimore, 1967), 225.

Limited Use of Force

Force need not be applied in battle and bloody conquest. Throughout history it has been, in countless cases, effective as a threat, even when not actually applied. What we witness, then, is not disappearance of force, but the tendency to modify its use.

In international relationships the wide spectrum of this modified, modulated or limited use of force begins where the threats of psychological warfare are unleashed against an opponent or a victim. It passes in an ascending curve from subversion to wars of national liberation, and it ends with limited wars of the Vietnam type. In examining the many cases within this wide range of uses of force which current history presents to us, we come upon two types of limited use of force which merit our special attention—confrontation and intervention.

Confrontation and intervention, the two types of use of force short of war, the subject of the present study, were instruments of foreign policy long before modern times and the dawn of the nuclear age. Yet, they have acquired new dimensions, and as words, at least partly new meanings. They are forms of use of force for achieving national goals. The degree of pressure applied is more or less carefully adapted to what the situation, as it appears to the factors, will bear without degenerating into an unwanted armed conflict. The two types of maneuver on the international scene have much in common, whereas in many respects they also differ widely. Their importance and their potentialities reside in the fact that, in opposition to what many superficial observers seem to assume, they are designed to avoid the higher and more dangerous levels of violence in cases where a nation deems it necessary to resort to force.

These two types of limited use of force are not only conceptually related insofar as they represent methods of bringing about change—or trying to bring about change—without war or serious risk of war. Confrontation in many instances may be a preliminary step. When confrontation does not yield the results expected by the power initiating it, such power can step up the confrontation so that it grows into intervention—always on condition, of course, that the relationship is such that intervention becomes possible. The Gulf of Tonkin confrontation of August 4, 1964, which was one of the steps on the ladder to all-out intervention in Vietnam, can be cited as an example. In that way, intervention may be considered as a development, as escalation of confrontation.

On the other hand, intervention can naturally develop without any preceding confrontation. Then the order may be reversed. Out of the intervention, involving as a rule a smaller and a much more powerful nation, a confrontation may result. This is the case where another great power tries to intervene on its own, or tries to protect the victim of intervention. Then we find confrontation within a situation of intervention, as was the case in the Congo in 1960. Or else an international, collective intervention may be substituted for an individual intervention, with the view to prevent a confrontation from developing, as was the case in the Dominican Republic in 1965.

In the course of the present study, which is concerned with the limited use of force by nations large or small, the two world powers, the United States of America and the Soviet Union will quite naturally play a predominant role. We witness how they use the same instruments of power politics such as diplomacy, propaganda, negotiations, foreign aid, alliance-building, threat of force, subversion. In spite of this similarity of the instruments, of tactics and techniques of their use, the two players must not be looked upon as perfectly symmetrical powers, both simply competing for the dominant position. Their motivations, their social and power structures, their outlook on the world is too different. Without qualifying in any way their respective ideologies, it is safe to say that they are irreconcilable.

Whereas in the United States peace has always been considered as the normal state of affairs and conflict an exception to be overcome at the earliest date, whether this conflict be domestic or international, the rulers of the Soviet Union profess to an entirely different belief. For the Soviet Union conflict—class struggle, struggle between the socialist and the capitalist system, war of national liberation—is the normal, desirable and permanent state of affairs. This is continually repeated in official statements. Even the concept of peaceful coexistence is synonymous with undying struggle. It implies that two antagonistic world systems exist which cannot be reconciled, and since reconciliation is neither possible nor desirable, they may provisionally try for tactical reasons to postpone a clash which in the long view is inevitable.

Such profound difference of outlook permeates the relationship between the two world powers and the relations between those powers and the smaller nations. This must not be lost from sight even when one deals, for the sake of convenience, with the two world powers as with symmetrical, comparable units.

Chapter II
The Concept Of Confrontation

Evolution of Terminology

The use of the word "Confrontation" to describe a specific kind of strategic situation within the wide spectrum of limited use of force, short of war, is equivalent to some kind of semantic usurpation. Confrontation is an old word with a wide variety of meanings. When it was first used in medieval Latin it was used primarily to describe a situation in which two opponents or two opposing concepts stood facing each other, *adversis frontibus* as classic Latin would have expressed it, in a hostile attitude. In the 16th century the term "to confront" meant to stand, or meet, or face in hostility or defiance, to present a bold front. Gradually the term acquired a much wider, more diffuse meaning. Today it seems to describe any situation where opposing elements meet, a situation, so to speak, where one has to stop, look and listen in order to make a decision. We are "confronted" with a choice, a question, a threat, an obstacle, a fact. We also "confront" two views in order to compare them.

Modern political terminology as it has developed since World War II has endowed the term "Confrontation" with a narrower, more specific meaning. This does not exclude the continued use of the term in its wide and general sense, as set out above, to which no one should object. However, the term has also acquired a special meaning due to its frequent use in the context of the study of problems of world power relationships and the study of the cold war. Thus, Herman Kahn uses the word to describe the situation of large Soviet and American strategic forces facing each other when he writes:

> The existing permanent alert of U.S. and Soviet strategic forces is an almost continual global confrontation.

13

He goes on to sketch specific scenarios of confrontations as follows:

> Tensions can build up further, and there may be limited but dramatic military confrontations, either local (as, for example, at the Brandenburg Gate) or global. Such confrontations are direct tests of nerve, committal, resolve, and recklessness. They are also dramatic enough to make all the participants and observers take note of what has happened. . . However, the main purpose of such confrontations, in addition to showing the resolve mentioned above, is to indicate clearly that reasonably large acts of violence are possible, . . .[1]

President John F. Kennedy applied the term in an equally wide, yet precise way, which seems most appropriate when it describes a particular situation in international relations. In his televised speech of July 25, 1961 on Berlin, the President said:

> West Berlin. . . has now become as never before, the great testing place of Western will and courage, a focal point where our solemn commitments. . . and Soviet ambitions now meet in basic confrontation.[2]

President Richard M. Nixon used the word "Confrontation" in a narrower sense, almost as an equivalent to the term cold war as characterized by rivalry and mutual pressures between two super-powers. When he spoke before the North Atlantic Council in Brussels on February 24, 1969, he expressed the view that "we are ending a period of confrontation and entering an era of negotiation."

In a study of crisis management, Alastair Buchan[3] described as "Confrontations" situations of the cold war in which the conflict approached a crisis, or in which it went through a series of crises of varying intensity. Similarly Louis J. Halle in his monumental *Cold War as History*[4] considered the Berlin blockade of 1948 to 1949 to be the first "Confrontation" of the Cold War, followed by others.

Thus the concept of "Confrontation" has assumed quite clear contours. When used in the context of the study of events

---

[1] Herman Kahn, *On Escalation, Metaphors and Scenarios* (New York, 1965), 74.

[2] *Documents on American Foreign Relations 1961* (New York: Council on Foreign Relations, 1962), 97.

[3] Alastair Buchan, *Crisis Management, The New Diplomacy,* Atlantic Paper (Paris, 1966), 40.

[4] Louis J. Halle, *The Cold War as History* (London, 1967), 166.

which occurred in the historic period between 1947 and 1969, it concerns the relationship of the Soviet Union and the United States of America at the points when such relationship grows critical and when decisions of importance have to be made on either side. On the other hand, "Confrontation" as a term continues to be used in a much looser, very wide meaning. A typical case in point is the discussion on July 24, 1959, between Richard Nixon, then Vice-President of the United States, and Chairman Khrushchev at the opening of the American industrial exhibition in Moscow, commonly referred to as "kitchen confrontation."

For the purpose of this book we suggest a use of the term which is somewhere between the two extremes. We define "Confrontation" as a situation when some form of a limited use or threat of force in international relationships is answered by an opponent with a symmetrical threat. Both opponents are compelled, in the course of the act, to stop, to think, and to make a new dicision. It is the essence of the concept that it implies something new and unusual, a basic change in the existing state of the relationship. The break in previous behavior is, as it is in the case of intervention, an important element. Decision will be based on the assessment of the opponent's resolve, nerve and determination, his physical strength on the spot, his overall strength, on the likelihood of escalation of the conflict, the effects on third parties and their possible reactions and whether they would be harmful, and finally, on the possibilities of ending the confrontation and returning to normal or near normal.

An able definition is proposed by Charles W. Koburger in *Military Review* where he writes:

> At its most abstract, a confrontation is the opposing of one or more elements of power with other elements of power, usually including some increment of military power, the object being to prevent the first party from succeeding in whatever it set out to do without actually applying violence. Confrontation's aim is to prevent an undesired action, by threat.[5]

---

[5] Lieutenant Commander Charles W. Koburger, Jr., "Komer's War. The Indirect Strategy in Action." *Military Review*, vol. 49, No. 8, (Fort Leavenworth. Kansas, 1969), 19.

Basically, "Confrontation," in this meaning of the term, is an exercise in deterrence. One party, after applying pressure in order to achieve a certain goal, meets with resistance designed to deter it from going further to make its threat come true. The possible losses which the first party risks incurring by continuing its course and by increasing pressures are demonstrated to it by the second party. The latter, in turn, may increase his demonstration to a point where the first party feels threatened and deploys his own instruments of dissuasion. Both parties are now placed in the position of the deterrer *and* deterred: They have to find out what their best interests dictate, to resolve either to go ahead in spite of the risks involved or to back down and find a means of extricating themselves from a difficult and dangerous entanglement which threatens to become too dangerous—and which may lead to war.

What is true for deterrence is also true for confrontation: When deterrence is effective and no armed conflict develops, we cannot know for sure what has been avoided or how serious the danger of war has really been. Equally, in confrontation, when both parties back down and extricate themselves from the situation they have created, it is difficult to decide what was really intended and how strong the resolve to achieve it had been.

Confrontation may also be viewed as an exercise in bargaining—tacit or explicit. It is the culmination of a process of negotiation where current communication, signals, gestures, deployment of force, or intervention of mediators and other third parties is exhausted and does not seem to promise any better outcome. Thomas C. Schelling describes this point in the following words:

> The final outcome must be a point from which neither expects the other to retreat; yet the main ingredient of this expectation is what one thinks the other expects the first to expect. . .[6]

We will, in the following chapters, meet with different kinds or classes of confrontations. They may be distinguished according to the instruments of power deployed or at least assumed to be decisive, they may be distinguished according to the type and category of the nations involved, or they may be

---

[6] Thomas C. Schelling, *The Strategy of Conflict* (New York, 1963), 70.

distinguished according to the degree of intensity of the clash of wills.

We shall, for our purpose, exclude from the realm of confrontation all clashes of political will in the international field where such clashes are not visibly and tangibly backed by a military threat or at least the likelihood of the involvement of armed force. For this type of political conflict many terms come to mind, among them the word "containment." Containment became a standard term in the context of the cold war when it was used by George Kennan in a paper prepared in January 1947. This paper became famous when it was published in *Foreign Affairs* in July 1947, as the *"Mr. X article."* In Kennan's own later interpretation the term meant simply a method of limiting conflict by an attitude which does not consider war as inevitable, a method of ceasing to make unilateral concessions to the Kremlin, a method of inspiring and supporting resistance against the Kremlin's efforts to expand the area of its dominant political influence, and a method of waiting for the internal weaknesses of Soviet power to moderate Soviet ambitions and behavior.[7] Thus, containment comes close to confrontation in the sense that it is a method of resistance in a political contest without recourse to violence, but since the military element is absent, it is not really confrontation.

Instruments and Subjects

In classifying confrontation according to the instruments of power involved, the first group which distinguishes itself clearly from the diffuse backdrop of other classes of confrontation is of course thermonuclear confrontation. Unless we accept Herman Kahns suggestion that the fact that American targets are zeroed in by Soviet missiles, and Soviet targets by American missiles is an almost continual global confrontation, it seems doubtful whether nuclear or thermonuclear confrontation ever really occurred in the course of the cold war years.

The nearest we have come to such a dramatic situation was probably the period of the U-2 incident in May 1960. One may

---

[7] George F. Kennan, *Memoirs 1925-1950* (London, 1968), 364, 367.

assume that at that time the United States had intensified its routine reconnaissance or espionage flights over Russia in view of the summit conference scheduled for May 15, 1960 in Paris. In circumstances analogous to the negotiations the Japanese had conducted in 1941 to hide their intentions of making a surprise attack, the American government may have felt that increased watchfulness was mandatory. When President Eisenhower refused to present excuses and to undertake the commitments demanded by the Soviet side, Chairman Khrushchev, in a press conference in Paris on May 18, threatened shattering blows against the foreign bases from which the U-2 planes operated. The situation indeed seemed close to a nuclear confrontation. This was emphasized by the alert given to the American strategic forces throughout the world and by the assumption that the government of the United States, deprived of the intelligence data normally provided by the U-2 flights, and under the added impression of the threatening remarks made by Khrushchev and later in Moscow by Marshall Malinowski, was deeply concerned and determined not to be taken by surprise.

Another instance of nuclear near-confrontation was the experimental explosion of Soviet multi-megaton warheads in the summer of 1961. This underlined the threat against Berlin. The United States retaliated by the resumption of its own atmospheric tests of nuclear devices.

As examples of what we may call conventional confrontations we can cite the Berlin blockade of 1948-1949, the building of the Berlin wall in 1961, the Cuban missile crisis in 1962, the Gulf of Tonkin incident in 1964, and the *Pueblo* incident in 1968. These were conventional in spite of the fact that at least one, sometimes both of the opponents were backed by their own nuclear panoplies, because the decision was brought about without any display of nuclear weapons.

If we distinguish between different types of confrontation according to the type and category of the nations involved, we think, of course, in the first place of the clashes of will between the world powers, the United States, the Soviet Union and China. China in this context may indeed be added to the group. These confrontations can be nuclear or conventional. They are distinguished from confrontations between pairs of smaller nations, or between a great power and a smaller nation, by the increased fear they generate. Since these powers are in possession of nuclear armaments, the risk involved seems to most observers greater than in the case of nations without such arms. This assumption hardly stands up to thorough scrutiny. Many safeguards are built into the mutual relationship of nuclear powers which promise to prevent the situation from getting out of hand. The most powerful of the safeguards, of course, is the risk of escalation of the conflict into a large nuclear exchange, which it is in the highest interest of all concerned to avoid. Such is the care with which the mutual relationship of force is being handled, and such are the anxieties generated that, when great powers are involved, it is less likely to reach even a stage which may be called confrontation than in the intercourse between lesser nations.

It is more likely, therefore, that situations between smaller powers—equals or near equals—will degenerate so much that a stage is reached which may be termed a confrontation in the full sense of the word. Examples are the conflicts between Indonesia and Malaysia, between the Philippines and Malaysia, between India and Pakistan, between Rhodesia and the United Kingdom, between Israel and Arab governmental and guerrilla forces, between Algeria and Morocco and between Portugal and its African neighbors. These are more likely to escalate beyond confrontation and into war than the great power confrontations, since the very limited power of the nations involved will encourage either one to believe that it may win a relatively easy military victory. Such beliefs have proved to be erroneous most of the time. Yet, in these antagonisms, the stabilizing factor which influences the relationship between heavily armed and well-organized societies are missing, so that the confrontation between smaller nations becomes almost equivalent to war. War, when it occurs, will, because of the limitations inherent in weak nations, naturally be limited—"limited," of course, in the sense of local limitation and the military technology applied, but not necessarily in losses, human suffering and general destruction, as the example of the war between Biafra and Nigeria shows.

And in the background, of course, always looms the danger of a great power involvement, which would place such limited conflicts on a different level where they would become a concern for the whole world.

Soviet Views

It would be difficult to trace in Soviet strategic doctrine a similar concept of confrontation. This is explained by the very elements of Soviet strategic thinking. Confrontation presupposes a certain symmetry between the opponents and cannot, therefore, be visualized by Soviet thinking as a special form of limited use of force in a conflict by some form of fleeting tacit agreement. Any common interest of the socialist and the capitalist world, even the common interest to avoid war, is unacceptable to the communist mind.[8] Communist ideology cannot visualize Russia's policy otherwise than aimed at achieving the final aims of this ideology. Thus it must be understood as permanently on the move forward, whereas "imperialism" and "capitalism" must be understood to be receding. Hence the total absence of the possibility of recognizing any similarity between its own position and that of an opponent. Confrontation, meaning a situation in which both opponents must stop their movements, would, in addition, be in direct contradiction to the dynamic view of Soviet strategy.

Equally, the very idea of mutual deterrence has never officially been accepted by Moscow. Since the Soviet Union is, as Moscow asserts, peaceful and does not plan any attack or aggression, it does not need to be deterred. The imperialist camp, on the other hand, according to Soviet doctrine, is permanently bent on the destruction of the Soviet fatherland and is only prevented from putting its plans into effect by the superior watchfulness and skill of Soviet diplomacy, backed, of course, by its superior military technology and by the determination of the peoples, even in the West, not to tolerate any aggressive move

---

[8] Curt Gasteyger, "Krieg und Abrüstung in sowjetischer Sicht," *Strategie und Abrüstungspolitik der Sowjetunion, Ausgewählte sowjetische Studien und Reden* (Frankfurt M.: Forschungsinstitut der Deutschen Gesellschaft für Auswärtige Politik, 1964), 46.

against the fatherland of Socialism. According to Soviet doctrine, "arms are the material instruments for waging war, and are being bought and developed in order to be used."[9] Hence the Western views on the stabilizing effect of the mutual thermonuclear threat are not shared, and a general war between imperialism and socialism with a massive exchange of atomic warheads is presented to the public as a possibility and even probability. Any situation coming near confrontation, as we see it, would, in Russian eyes, inevitably escalate into the dreaded all-out war, in which capitalism would lose and socialism triumph.

To avoid war is in the interest of the peoples of this world, according to Soviet theory, and peaceful coexistence is the only way to accomplish it. Recognition of the principle of peaceful coexistence is equivalent not only to renunciation of war as the use of force against another state, but also to renunciation of a policy apt to lead to war. Consequently, the Soviet Union insists on general and complete disarmament, with the tacit understanding that such force as remains in the world will obey historical necessity and work automatically for the achievement of the ultimate goals of Moscow.

Peaceful coexistence, in Soviet theory, is a form of limiting the use of force and the risk of war in an existing and continuing contest between opposing interests. It comes, therefore, as close as possible to what we describe as the necessity to limit conflict and includes, so to say, the system of confrontation.

"Our Time"

In order to define the period of recent history which we may, for the purpose of the forthcoming investigation, call "our time," we propose to choose, among the many dates which offer themselves to the observer, the year 1947 for a beginning. That year was marked by events which had decisive influence on the course of future developments: Independence of India, initiation of the reconstruction of Europe under the Marshall Plan, failure of the American effort to save China from communism, the

---

[9] W. A. Sorin, P. F. Schachow, A. N. Schewtschenko, "Die Unhaltbarkeit der westlichen Abschreckungstheorie," *Strategie und Abrüstungspolitik der Sowjetunion,* loc. cit., 200.

Truman doctrine, and the setting of a course away from re-unification of Germany.

The number of situations which come close to our definition of confrontation, in the course of the twenty-three years elapsed since 1947, is curiously enough equal to the number of years elapsed since 1947—twenty-three situations in twenty-three years. It remains, of course, open to debate which events really correspond to the definition and which among the countless controversies and clashes of interest, which naturally mark the path of sovereign nations and the intercourse of governments, are important enough to be considered, and which others, on the other hand, are too important or rather so violent that they transcend confrontation and must be called wars. In some cases we will find that in a war elements of confrontation were included.

A summary list of confrontations in that period would include the Berlin blockade of 1948-1949, the situation existing between the People's Republic of China and the Republic of China (Formosa) after 1949, the Suez crisis of 1956, the conflict between Honduras and Nicaragua in 1957, the conflict between Spain and Morocco from 1957 to 1958, the Ladak incidents between China and India in 1959, the Berlin ultimatum of 1959, the U-2 incident of 1960, the Congo crisis beginning in 1960 and the attempt to destroy the United Nations of the same year, the border clashes between Somalia and Ethiopia from 1960 to 1964, the Bizerte incident of 1961, the building of the Berlin wall in 1961, the Cuban missile crisis of 1962, the annexation of New Guinea by Indonesia in the same year, the Chinese attack on India in October 1962, the Indonesian-Malaysian clash from 1963 to 1965, the conflict between Morocco and Algeria in 1963, the pressures exercised against Portuguese Guinea from 1963 to 1968, and against Mozambique and Angola throughout this period, the clashes between Kenya and Somalia from 1963 to 1967, the Cyprus crises of 1964 and 1967, the outbreak of hostilities between India and Pakistan in 1965, the pressures of Spain on Gibraltar, the clashes between China and the Soviet Union of 1969.

A first glance at this summary list already reveals one noteworthy fact: In only six of the twenty-three situations listed above were the world powers directly involved, and in five of these no armed force was actually used. In all of the remaining cases but one—Gibraltar—shots were fired in anger and some ascended to a level which came close to all-out war.

Chapter III

Confrontation In Our Time – Part One

Berlin I - the Blockade

The first great confrontation of our time grew out of the deep cleavage in the attitudes of the great powers with respect to the future of defeated Germany. In promoting the Marshall Plan the United States, eagerly supported by the nations of Western Europe, had set the course. The economy of Europe, shattered by the world war, was to be rebuilt; the widespread misery which was thought to be the most favorable breeding ground for communism was to be overcome. In this effort of reconstruction, the former enemies were to be included.

In 1947, the policy of military occupation, of isolation of the different parts of Germany, of dismantling industries, of perpetuating economic chaos was reversed by the West. The British and the American zones of occupation, by an agreement of December 2, 1946, were joined to form one economic unit, the Bi-zone. In an agreement of June 3, 1948, France agreed to add its zone of occupation. A foreign ministers' conference of the United States, the Soviet Union, Great Britain and France in London from November 25 through December 15, 1947, could not reach agreement on the principles of a peace treaty for the whole of Germany. It failed mainly because of disagreement over immoderate Soviet and French territorial and economic claims.

The Western powers decided to go it alone and convened on February 3, 1948 in London in a conference, to which they invited the three Benelux states, but not the Soviet Union. In protest, Moscow withdrew its representative from the Allied Control Council in Berlin on March 20, 1948. As a first measure to be taken jointly in the three western zones and independently from the Soviets, a currency reform in Germany was instituted on June 21, 1948. The Germans were invited at the same time to build governmental institutions of their own in the three western zones which now formed a unit, and a Parliamentary Council (*Parlamentarischer Rat*) was set up.

As a consequence of the cessation of the four-power regime in the whole of Germany on March 20, 1948, the Soviet Union declared that the division of Germany was now a fact, and that therefore traffic between the Soviet zone of occupation and the Western zones, and between Berlin and the West had to be drastically reduced. When the West insisted on currency reform, the Soviet Government took it as a reason for declaring that the Western powers had forfeited their right to occupy their sectors in Berlin, and that these sectors were part of their zone in Germany. Consequently, they tightened the blockade which had been initiated on April 1st, and on June 25th they cut off all food, coal, and other supplies, including electricity, from the area under their control to West Berlin, and they stopped all surface traffic. For technical reasons the water supply was not interrupted. The Soviets simultaneously introduced a currency reform in their zone of occupation and prohibited the import and possession of the new western currency. In reply, the West made the Deutsche Mark (DM) the only legal tender in West Berlin.

Suddenly, a true confrontation of will was now upon the governments. On June 21, 1948, the Western powers began to supply by air the population of their sectors in the blockaded city. They set up a complete air lift by transport planes, which was to go on for months, day and night, until the blockade was lifted. During the air lift's ten months duration, 1.5 million tons of goods were ferried to Berlin by 380 airplanes in a total of nearly 200,000 flights. On June 30, 1948, the American Secretary of State, General George Marshall and the British Foreign Minister, Ernest Bevin, announced the West's determination to insist on their rights, based on the Potsdam agreement, to be in and to remain in Berlin.

The stakes in this contest of resolve between East and West were much higher than the right to occupy a few dozen square kilometers in Berlin. The contest was to decide the future of Germany: Whether it was to grow into a free and prosperous society, or whether it would be kept under some form of military and police regime and in permanent misery analogous to the peoples of the Soviet Union and of those under her domination. The outcome would decide, moreover, whether Western Europe would be reconstructed, under the umbrella of relative security provided by the military might of the United States of America, or whether it would be left to an uncertain fate.

In this confrontation of truly historical dimensions and import, the strategic balance seemed at the outset to be overwhelmingly weighted in favor of the Soviet Union. Berlin was separated by 150 kilometers of land solidly in the hands of the Soviet armies. The British and American forces of occupation in Germany were widely scattered as a kind of police force and were not combat ready in any respect. It was almost a year before the first results of an effort to regroup and equip them as an effective, though small, fighting force became visible. The American, British and French garrisons in West Berlin were not much more than token forces.

The American Commander, General Lucius Clay, and the highest magistrate of Berlin, Ernest Reuter, then *Regierender Bürgermeister,* were of the opinion that the closing of land communications was only a bluff to test the West's resolve and had recommended, as early as March 1948 that the bluff be called by opening the Autobahn by an armed convoy. In view of the extreme weakness of the American forces in the theater, President Truman reluctantly decided not to try the test which might have led to an armed clash.[1] A threat with atomic weapons, which might have accompanied the limited ground operation, was discarded as unpracticable, since the risk that use of such weapons would precipitate a general war was not considered proportionate to the object to be defended.

---

[1] Gerhard Wettig, *Entmilitarisierung und Wiederbewaffnung in Deutschland 1943-1955* (München, 1967), 219.

The expensive and, at the outset uncertain, expedient of the airlift was suggested and had to be adopted. It was the first instance—many more were to come—in which the American leadership was presented with the fact that insufficient conventional strength on the spot could prevent even a world power in possession of a nuclear monopoly from the most limited, and probably effective, deployment of force on the spot.

Why did the Soviet Union not make use of this favorable conjuncture? Could Stalin not assume that Soviet occupation of Berlin by force would persuade the West to agree to the inclusion of Berlin in the Soviet held part of Germany; and could he not assume that, as a bonus, the West would be ready to enter into other arrangements favorable to Russia?

Some of the reasons for moderation may have been political, others strategic. There are grounds for speculating that, even if such a speculation credits Soviet policy with a subtleness which it rarely exhibits, Stalin did not really want to take the whole of Berlin. He may have found it more favorable to tolerate this vulnerable and weak outpost of the West, where pressure could easily be brought to bear, and with the help of which he could hope finally to discourage and divide the Western allies and to create deep divisions within Germany.

An obvious strategic reason for not pressing the issue was that the United States had the atomic bomb, whereas the Soviet Union would not conduct its first nuclear explosion until more than a year later, in September 1949.[2] The means of delivery of the atomic bomb at that time was the obsolescent B-29 bomber of World War II fame. Sixty of these bombers were moved at once to Great Britain. With their limited range they could reach from East Anglia inside the Soviet Union as far as Moscow and return to their base or to some base on the continent. As a consequence of this crisis, air-to-air refueling was introduced for these bombers.[3] The West's outward show of determination, represented by the tacit and never overt atomic threat, probably effectively deterred the Soviet Union from such

---

[2] Announced by President Harry S. Truman on September 23, 1949.

[3] Arnold A. Rogow, *James Forrestal, A Study of Personality, Politics and Policy* (New York, 1963), 207.

drastic steps as forcible occupation of the Western sectors of Berlin.

The question, of course, arises, what would have happened in this first great confrontation of the Cold War had it occurred two years later, when Russia's ruler was in possession of at least a few atomic bombs as well as the airplanes capable of delivering them over a short distance? The answer is that the West would have been still more reluctant to use its weak ground forces even in a limited way, and the Soviets would not have used their weak nuclear arms, even as a threat. Therefore, the situation would have remained much the same. As later confrontations show, the possession of nuclear armaments by both sides has always, so far, prevented the use of conventional military force.

We recognize in this confrontation a typical case of tacit bargaining, interspersed with declarations and some explicit negotiations. As Thomas C. Schelling points out in his *Strategy of Conflict,* tacit agreement requires "terms that are qualitatively distinguishable from the alternative." The participants must be ready "to allow the situation itself to exercise substantial constraint to accept some dictation from the elements themselves."[4] The tacit agreement reached over Berlin was that no attempt should be made by the West to open the ground corridors by forcible means and no interference by the Soviet Union was to take place with the air corridors leading to Berlin. Both kinds of interference with the other's rights would have been technically and tactically feasible, and it is doubtful whether either would have precipitated a wider conflict. Yet the situation was such that no graduated application of countermeasures was possible. Ground closed, air open was an easily distinguishable situation, whereas any other proposition would have been ambiguous and, therefore, might have de-stabilized the situation. Similarly, attention of the world had been so much fixed on this strange island Berlin, so conspicuous in the red sea, that on both sides the conviction must have existed that its removal would be deeply de-stabilizing and would open the door to

---

[4] Thomas C. Schelling, *The Strategy of Conflict* (New York, 1963), 75.

completely unforeseeable and probably unwanted developments. As Schelling puts it:

> Once the contingency is upon them, their interests, which originally diverged in the play of threats and deterrents, substantially coincide in the desperate need for a focus of agreement.[5]

An agreement was reached on May 12, 1949 in a New York conference of the Foreign Ministers of the four powers involved in the Berlin confrontation. The Soviet Union removed all impediments against free circulation and trade between West Berlin and the zone occupied by the Soviet armies, and between that zone and the area which a fortnight later was to become the Federal Republic of Germany. The West in turn removed the counter measures introduced earlier. The confrontation was ended by the defeat of the side which had started it, the Soviet Union.

This confrontation over Berlin at an end, the problems dividing the powers remained. The same confrontation recurred nine years later in different forms and places, when it was carried to Paris and to Cuba.

Suez 1956

The next confrontation which was soon to shake the world was of quite another character. In it, the world powers and two major European powers were involved in an array quite different from the usual front lines of the Cold War. When the dust had settled over the scene, one could clearly see that the relationships between the nations involved would never be the same again. It was the Suez crisis.

It all began with the agreement of October 19, 1954 between Egypt and Great Britain, in which the latter renounced its treaty rights to maintain a military basis on the Suez Canal and to assume its defense. Egypt was now in full physical possession of the international waterway and determined to use it as an instrument in its bargaining with East and West about the much needed support for its monumental plan of development, the Aswan High Dam. The success of this gigantic feat of engineering was planned to be the consecration of Egypt's

---

[5] *ibid.*, 80.

leading role in the Arab world and of the dominant position of its dictator, Colonel Gamal Abdel Nasser.

Egypt initially had turned to Great Britain and the United States for help in this project. Since the experts in the two countries, for technological and economic reasons, had reservations against the plan, Abdel Nasser sought assistance in Moscow. Now, alarmed that in the wake of the colossal undertaking the Soviet Union might deeply penetrate the Middle East and finally replace western influence, Washington and London reversed their course. On December 17, 1955, they offered their conditional support to Egypt. Seven months later, after lengthy negotiations, Egypt accepted the offer. On July 20, in a *volte-face* typical of the inconsistency of American policy of the Eisenhower years, the offer was withdrawn by the United States and the United Kingdom.

It was a severe blow to Colonel Nasser's prestige—and it was planned as such a blow. However, Abdel Nasser retaliated by using the most effective weapon in his possession, his power over the Suez Canal. On July 26, 1956, by decree of the Egyptian government, the *Compagnie Universelle du Canal de Suez* was nationalized, expropriated and dissolved. The West, under the leadership of Secretary of State John Foster Dulles, did not defend its legal rights, based on agreements freely entered into by the interested parties in 1854, 1866, 1888, 1954, but tried by subtle legalistic procedures and face-saving devices, worked out in a conference in London, to keep at least the international waterway open and in good state of repair. Meetings of the British, French and Egyptians in the office of the Secretary General of the United Nations, held between October 13 and 19, finally promised an arrangement acceptable to the parties most concerned.

This hopeful development was interrupted on October 29, 1956, by an attack by Israeli forces in the Sinai peninsula. The attack grew out of a long series of incidents and clashes between Egyptian and Israeli forces along the armistice line, but it had been strongly encouraged by France and was actually supported by France with air and naval forces. France had felt especially frustrated by the seizure of the canal since the company exercising ownership and exploiting the waterway was located in Paris. Moreover it was known that the rebellion in Algeria received massive support and encouragement from Cairo. As early as July 31, 1956, France had offered Great Britain military cooperation for an intervention against Egypt. Gradually Paris succeeded in winning the weak British government under Anthony Eden for an operation in the old imperialistic style, for which London still hoped to get American support. In August common planning was begun for an operation which might later be decided upon, and sizable French and British amphibious forces were deployed in Cyprus and Malta.

While the Security Council of the United Nations, meeting at the request of the United States, was still considering the aggression by Israel, the governments of France and Britain issued, on October 30, an ultimatum to Egypt and Israel. They demanded that the opponents withdraw their forces from the Suez Canal—Israel had none in the vicinity of the waterway—and asked Egypt to agree to the stationing of French and British forces on important points along the canal. When these demands were ignored some ineffective air attacks were made against Egypt. On the morning of November 2, French and British landings began in the area of Port Said.

So far, it had been an operation to be described as intervention in the domestic affairs of one nation, Egypt, disguised as intervention in a war in order to separate the combatants and to establish peace. However, it now became a confrontation of will, resolve and power in the full extent of the word.

The United States, eager to win or regain the gratitude and affection of the new nations in the developing world, and motivated, one may assume, by oil interests as well as by the concept of an international legal order, immediately brought the case before the world forum of the United Nations. When the Security Council could not exercise its responsibility because of lack of unanimity, it called, on October 31, 1956, an emergency special session of the General Assembly, under the terms of the 1950 *Uniting for Peace* Resolution.

Britain and France were now confronted by a wide array of power, of governments determined to force the withdrawal of the intervening troops and confident that they could achieve this by other means than force. For many reasons, France and its ally found themselves, from the very beginning, in a weak position. First, they had interrupted promising negotiations by a unilateral act and, in so doing, put themselves in the position of an aggressor, losing their former stance as the aggrieved party which could justly allege that Egypt had broken a whole series of treaties and agreements. Secondly, their military action was carried out too slowly with a force too small to deter Egyptian resistance. Overwhelming strength might have warranted an unopposed or almost unopposed landing and might have prevented serious fighting. Third, force was applied after a delay of seven days after the ultimatum and at a moment when the General Assembly was already meeting in emergency session. This was a challenge to the international body, and an outrage to world opinion. The opponents of this act were already conveniently gathered and in a position to act swiftly. Fourth, Britain found herself in opposition to almost all members of the then still existing Commonwealth and risked breaking up this loose association in the process. British domestic public opinion was deeply divided, and opposition to Eden's course threatened a major political crisis. The "special relationship" with the United States was at stake. Fifth, the two generally antagonistic world powers were for once to be found in the same camp, both determined to resist the aggression. The effect of this unique situation was to be increased vis-a-vis France and the United Kingdom by the inclination of both world powers to outdo the other in the eyes of the developing world in eagerness to protect the legal order. Despite its involvement in a dangerous conflict caused by the Hungarian uprising, or perhaps moved by a situation in which crisis had compelled removal of restraint, the Soviet Union assumed a particularly threatening attitude. In a letter from Marshal Bulganin to Guy Mollet, the then President of the Council of Ministers, the following ominous words appeared: "The Soviet Government is fully determined to apply force in order to crush the aggressors and restore peace in the East." And in a letter to Prime Minister Anthony Eden he wrote: "There are countries which need not have sent a navy or air force to the coasts of Britain but could have used other means, such as rocket technique."[6]

Technologically considered, this latter threat was probably premature since such techniques were not yet available, yet it was politically effective. It had a deep impact on public opinion in France and Britain and reinforced domestic resistance against the initiative of the two respective governments, which had been very strong from the outset on moral grounds.

In the light of the then existing missile technology it remains doubtful whether Bulganin could have made good his threat. In 1955 the Soviet Union had shown to the public two different types of heavy bombers with ranges of approximately ten thousand kilometers. It had been well known since 1952 that intercontinental ballistic missiles (ICBM) were being developed. By 1956 work must have been in an advanced stage, as the launching of the "Sputnik" on October 4, 1957, and a month later of a much heavier reentry vehicle, soon were to prove. A first short range missile with a range of two hundred kilometers came into service in 1957, and an intermediary range ballistic missile (IRBM) with a range of three thousand kilometers was operative in 1959. Yet, it seems doubtful whether any missiles able to reach London and Paris, other than prototypes flying a distance of one thousand kilometers, were ready for use in November, 1956.

However, the threat, combined with the political pressures already mentioned, worked. On December 22, 1956, the French and British had completed the withdrawal of their forces from the Suez Canal and a United Nations Emergency Force (UNEF), ordered to be created by the General Assembly on November 5, took their place. On March 8, 1957, Israel also withdrew all her forces from Egyptian territory.

The great confrontation was over. Two medium or great powers had yielded to the pressure of the world powers combined, acting through the United Nations, and backed by the overwhelming majority of all governments of the world. The decisive element, however, had been tacit agreement between

---

[6] Louis J. Halle, *The Cold War as History* (London, 1967), 341.

the world powers which, in this instance, did not neutralize one another, but rather brought to bear their combined weight.

Berlin II - the Ultimatum

The end of the first confrontation over Berlin in 1949 had not brought an end to its ordeal. It did not help the isolated city to cease to be a point of highest importance and a danger spot. On the contrary, we may assume that one of the motives which induced Stalin in 1949 to back down was the wish to keep this door open and to use it at a later and more favorable time. That time seemed to have come for Stalin's heir and successor in 1958.

The Soviet Union now had in its arsenal a few intercontinental ballistic missiles with a megaton re-entry vehicle, and a sizable number of short range missiles able to range as far as the Rhine and thereby threaten almost the whole of the Federal Republic of Germany with nuclear devastation. The conventional military posture was one of vast superiority over the still weak NATO ground forces. A medium range ballistic missile would be operative and in position sometime in 1959, and this could easily reach all the capitals of Western Europe.

President Eisenhower's probable attitude in a confrontation was forecast as one of a man deeply devoted to peace, and the mood of his surroundings was one of 'business as usual." The same held true for the Conservative government in Britain under Harold Macmillan. In France, General de Gaulle, recently ascended to power, had started a spectacular withdrawal from the military organization of NATO and a display of anti-Americanism. The political climate seemed favorable, the military superiority overwhelming.

Accordingly, Chairman Khrushchev opened his moves by an announcement on November 27, 1958 to the effect that, within six months, the Soviet Union would hand over the control of communications with Berlin to the authorities of the *Deutsche Demokratische Republik,* the DDR, and thereby end the four-power responsibility for Berlin and its roads of access. The announcement had been introduced by a threatening speech by Khrushchev and a corresponding article in "Pravda."

It was followed on December 11 by a statement to the effect that once this arrangement was made, and not later than within six months, any attempt by the Allies to force access to Berlin by armed convoys—the possibility considered and rejected in 1948—would be deemed to be a military attack on the DDR. Since this entity was placed under the protection of the Soviet Union, general war could hardly be avoided, with the full use of thermonuclear missiles it implied.

After consultation among each other and with the Federal Republic of Germany, the Western powers made their reply known on the last day of the year 1958. It was to the effect that they would not tolerate a unilateral modification of the existing agreements on Berlin, but would be willing to engage in negotiations as long as they included the whole of the problem of the division of Germany.

Moscow did not seem quite reassured about the attitude the United States would finally take. One of the Deputy Prime Ministers, Anastas Mikoyan, was sent on a "private" visit to the United States, and it was hinted that he was carrying important peace proposals. The visit was introduced by—or coincided with—a spectacular space experiment: A giant rocket fired by Soviet engineers at the moon passed the earth's satellite within a distance of less than seven thousand kilometers, to disappear in outer space. This happened after two American moon shots, attempted a little earlier, had failed. Mikoyan's mission was commented upon by the American press in an extravagant way, which seemed to indicate fear of Soviet rocket technology and an inordinate desire to maintain peace at any price.

President Eisenhower's remarks in his press conference on March 11, 1959 sounded reassuring to the Russians. He said that it was out of the question that the United States would fight a ground war in Europe, since they were clearly much inferior in conventional force on the spot. He added, however, that if the West was going to fight, it would be thermonuclear war in which the cities of the two contestants would be destroyed. Thus, he made the classical threat of massive retaliation.

It worked. Khrushchev did not want to go to such extremes. As the fateful date of May 27, 1959, approached, he began to hint that no ultimatum had been intended and that the date could be postponed for one, two or several months. In addition, a meeting of the heads of governments might be appropriate in which a settlement of the Berlin problem would be sought.

It is interesting to note that Khrushchev had now gained full control of the government of the Soviet Union. Bulganin had been deposed, and in December the head of police, General Serow, who had been very close to the head of government and party, was dismissed. It looked as if Khrushchev had attained full control with the help of the military, yet it was unclear how far he now depended on the generals, and how close they were willing to go to the brink of war under his unpredictable leadership.

Instead of accepting the idea of a meeting of heads of state, the West proposed to begin negotiations with a foreign minister's conference. The four ministers met in Geneva from May 11 to August 5, 1959. At Geneva the Soviets renewed practically all their former demands, including the withdrawal of the Western garrisons with the exception of small symbolic contingents, from Berlin. This demand was presented as a valuable concession by saying that the Soviet Union was willing to postpone the fulfillment of her conditions for a full year. The West could not accept such humiliating treatment. The conference ended in deadlock. It was the last of a long series of formal conferences dedicated to the problem of Germany. The increase of violence in the latter stage of the great confrontation made unthinkable a resumption of those four-power talks, which had originated in the war and which had been, for so many years in the postwar period such a natural and easy practice.

To veil his failure, the versatile Khrushchev made a new move. He asked for and got an invitation to visit President Eisenhower in Washington. The visit took place in September, 1959, and included three days of private talks with Eisenhower at his resting place, Camp David in Maryland. The spirit of the past confrontation seemed completely forgotten and the American—and world—public rejoyced in the expectation that the Cold War was over. The legendary "spirit of Camp David" was born.

Analysts well acquainted with Russian psychology have concluded that Khrushchev was sincere in his attempt to end the confrontation and to reach some sort of accommodation at that time. Louis J. Halle concludes in his book *The Cold War as History*:

> All this is not a dream. The record of the visit is there. Moreover, those who remember what had come before, and what was to come after, should not jump to the conclusion that Khrushchev was not, himself, genuinely moved by the good-will he expressed so warmly. Especially in the heart of a Russian, hate can pass over into love in an instant. Both emotions have a relationship to fear that makes them akin.[7]

The result of the bilateral talks in the United States was that Eisenhower accepted an invitation to the Soviet Union and agreed to a meeting of heads of state before the end of the year. The ultimatum and the date of May 27 were forgotten; the confrontation was ended, again without a result for the Soviets.

Khrushchev now met with sharp criticism by Peking of any compromise with the West. Eisenhower, in turn, was confronted with the refusal by France and the Federal Republic to negotiate the issue of Berlin as an isolated item; the two governments felt that in the weak position in which the West found itself, no concession was possible there without losing the hold on the city altogether. Only Great Britain was eager to negotiate and ready to accept accommodation at any price. In view of these difficulties, and the difficult negotiations within the two camps, the summit conference was postponed and finally set for May 16, 1960.

While the western powers continued to make a show of firmness in their position on Berlin, for the sake of self-respect and to keep the Federal Republic safely within the Alliance, they remained deeply divided over the goals to be pursued in their policy with respect to Germany. Yet things moved secretly within the Soviet orbit.

---

[7] *ibid.*, 366.

Relationships between Moscow and Peking were rapidly deteriorating. Khrushchev was held responsible for it. His critics could point to the much more daring policy of China, which had occupied Tibet without meeting with any resistance of the great powers, and was now starting to put pressure on India. The policy of confrontation over Berlin instead, in which Khrushchev had gone to the extreme of openly threatening nuclear war, had not brought any tangible result. He felt that he had soon to achieve success, lest he lose his grip on the conflicting elements on which his power was based—the army, the party, and the police. Plans had to be made to make the conference in Paris a success, either by dividing the opponents and thereby winning concessions or by converting it into the starting point for new pressures, a new confrontation.

Paris - the U-2

Actually, the Soviet ruler had no other choice. As the date of the summit approached, the attitude of France, the Federal Republic, and the United States made it more and more unlikely that they could easily be moved to back down on the issue of Berlin. On the contrary, they were more likely to insist on a general discussion of re-unification of Germany and the world-wide problems of disarmament under effective international inspection. The meeting threatened to end again in a draw, an outcome which would be most unfavorable to the position of Khrushchev. An unexpected incident came to his rescue, and he exploited it fully, and so much so, that the world seemed to come, once more, close to thermonuclear war.

On May 1st, 1960, one of the American U-2 reconnaissance airplanes, which had flown under contract with the Central Intelligence Agency and with civilian pilots, at high altitude over the Soviet Union, was shot down. This was revealed by Khrushchev on May 5, without saying, however, that the pilot had parachuted and was a prisoner, and without saying that the special sophisticated equipment of the airplane had been found and carefully studied by the appropriate services. Washington issued a statement, routine when a spy is caught hot-handed, which pretended that the lost plane was a weather plane operating along the Turkish border. In reply, Moscow revealed what they knew. President Eisenhower, aware of the fact that the American public and the world widely (and correctly) assumed that he was not fully informed on the activities of the American government and not really in control of it, could not help but insist that he had known of the reconnaissance flights all along and that he assumed full responsibility for them.

This put Khrushchev in a difficult position vis-a-vis his critics and opponents within the government circles. Meeting with Eisenhower in Paris in the spirit of Camp David, exhibiting the good-humored friendliness which was thought to be the right tactics for extricating concessions from the old General, would inevitably be interpreted by the enemies of the dictator to mean that Khrushchev was not in a position to defend the Soviet Union's vital interest against a cunning foe who was admittedly engaged in espionage of the most dangerous kind. At the same time it gave Khrushchev an instrument for extricating himself from an adventure—the summit conference—which showed less and less promise. The dictator could not face the possibility of returning from Paris without having achieved at least partly his aim to dislodge the Western powers from Berlin.

Therefore, Khrushchev, arriving earlier than scheduled at Paris, proposed to President de Gaulle that the first meeting of the summit conference should not be confidential and that the statements should be made public. This was accepted. President Eisenhower, President de Gaulle, Prime Minister Macmillan and Khrushchev met accordingly on May 16 at the Elysee Palace. Khrushchev immediately asked to read a statement. It was to the effect that the conference could not begin, and that he would not participate in it unless the United States publicly express their regret for the U-2 flights, promised to punish those responsible for them, and pledged not to continue them. Then he withdrew the invitation extended to Eisenhower to visit Moscow.

Eisenhower, who had, of course, been informed of what was to be expected, answered in a statement to the effect that the reconnaissance flights, in view of the constant Soviet threats of destroying other countries by nuclear missiles, regrettably had become an absolute necessity. He had come to Paris for nego- tiations which finally would make all espionage unnecessary. The flights had been discontinued, though, and would not be resumed. Yet, otherwise he could not accept the conditions set for opening the conference. The meeting adjourned after four hours, and the Russian and the American statements were made public.

On the following day, President de Gaulle, the host, called a plenary meeting of the conference. Eisenhower made it known that the Soviet demands and conditions would be deemed with- drawn if Khrushchev attended the session. This latter, however, did not show up and publicly declared that he stuck to his conditions. Thereupon de Gaulle, in his capacity as host to the affair, stated that the conference could not take place.

The following day, Khrushchev held a press conference. It was noted that throughout the whole trip to Paris and wherever he went, he was accompanied by the minister of defense, Mar- shall R. A. Malinowski, who was known not to be his friend and who, with a somber face, watched the antics of his master with- out uttering a word. In terms of unprecedented violence Khrushchev, in front of the press, attacked the United States and her President. He threatened that in the future all airplanes which might again be sent over the Soviet Union would be shot down, that the bases from which the planes operated would be destroyed and that those who had established them—i.e. the United States—would suffer shattering blows. This was obvious- ly also aimed at intimidating the nations which had allowed the United States to set up bases for intermediary range ballistic missiles intended to make up for the deficient number of inter- continental missiles then available and deployed. These nations were Great Britain, where four *Thor* bases existed, Italy, where two *Jupiter* bases were under construction, and Turkey, where one *Jupiter* base was projected.[8] He went on to say that the Soviet Union was now ready to sign any day a peace treaty with

---

[8] Each base had 15 missiles. *Thor* was a liquid fuelled IRBM, range 2400 kilometers, *Jupiter* also with liquid propellant, and of the same range.

the DDR, which, when signed, would deprive the Western powers of their right to keep occupation troops in West Berlin.

With these thundering threats resounding throughout the world, Khrushchev flew to East Berlin. Now, having extricated himself from an unpromising conference, he changed the tone of the confrontation. To the disappointment of the rulers in East Berlin he said in a public meeting—after affirming that the occupation of the Western sectors of the divided city would not be allowed to go on forever—that the Soviet Union would not contribute to any worsening of the situation. Therefore, he would maintain the *status quo* until a meeting of the heads of government in hopefully six-to-eight months time—which implied that it would be after the American presidential elections and with another president in the White House—could consider and settle the matter. As we know, this meeting never took place, and the *status quo* continued.

This narrative brings out the elements of confrontation contained in these dramatic days of May. Would President Eisenhower accept humiliation—apologies, pledges for further action, recall of a former invitation—in order to save the conference? Would the Allies split and put pressure to bear on the United States, in order to save the talks? Would Pakistan, Turkey and Norway, the countries between which the U-2 flights were apparently operating, show signs of trying to dissociate themselves from the United States? Would the United Kingdom, Italy and Turkey withdraw their permission to keep or set up IRBM bases on their territory? Such were the questions asked. The instruments of forcing a reply were the open and expressly made threats with nuclear destruction, accompanied with a show of strange, unpredictable behavior designed to arouse deep concern and anguish in the hearts of the opponents.

That the confrontation was really a nuclear confrontation in the minds of the two main opponents has been mentioned earlier. The United States was bracing herself for a nuclear surprise attack during the weeks preceding the summit meeting, and the leader of the Soviet Union—or his most influential advisers—were determined to go to the brink of nuclear war in order to break the will of the opponents and to disrupt the alliance of the West. The confrontation was called off when it appeared that it was not possible to change the *status quo* by means short of war.

It was followed only two months later by a new confrontation when the outbreak of a crisis in Africa—unexpected in the way events were chasing each other—made a new contest of will and resolve almost inevitable. Now the chance of gaining a decisive advantage over the opponents, the chance of a much needed victory, seemed to beckon to the hard-pressed Soviet ruler.

The Congo, 1960 - 1963

The crisis was of similar magnitude as the preceeding one, or perhaps even more important and threatening, when it evolved in the heart of Africa and spread to the World Organization in New York. Five days after the Congo was given independence by Belgium, on July 5, 1960, a mutiny broke out in the *force publique,* the former colonial army, which had now become the Congo's national army, and chaos developed in the few urban centers of the immense new state. Belgium moved in metropolitan forces in order to restore security. The subsequent events were really a series of interventions, the most important case of intervention in our time, lasting from July 10, 1960, to June 30, 1964, and they will be dealt with in a later chapter. However, within this intervention, an important confrontation between the world powers developed.

The very day on which the Security Council of the United Nations called upon Belgium to withdraw her forces and instructed the Secretary General to give the Congolese military assistance for the restoration of order and security, the Prime Minister of the Congo, Patrice Lumumba, appealed to the Soviet Union for military help against Belgium. The appeal letter bore the hallmark of the Soviet Foreign Ministry's documents, and was immediately answered by Khrushchev in a note full of recriminations against the western powers and their policy towards the Congo. It concluded with the pledge that the Soviet Union would not hesitate to take the most energetic measures to repel the aggressors. This was equivalent to a declaration of

intention to send Soviet forces to Africa. On July 13 the Foreign
Minister of the Soviet Union denounced the United States, the
United Kingdom, France, the Federal Republic of Germany and
Belgium for waging armed aggression against the Congo with
the purpose to destroy its independence. The reply was given by
the representative of the United States in a session of the Security Council in the night of July 20-21. He declared that the government of the United States would only tolerate the entry of
security forces of the United Nations in the Congo, and that the
United States, in union with other governments, was prepared
to prevent the penetration of foreign national forces with all
means at their disposal.

Several African governments, especially Liberia and Tunisia,
aware of the danger of a great power confrontation developing
in the heart of Africa, now brought pressure to bear on Lumumba, who, on July 22, suddenly withdrew his appeal to the Kremlin. Lumumba, under the strain of the domestic crisis, became
more and more inconsistent. One day he announced an appeal
for Russian help, another day he clamored for American troops.
The situation was met by the intervention of the United Nations
and an international force, which will be described later.

Renewed threats were uttered a few days later by Soviet
speakers when the provincial government of the Congolese
province of the Katanga manifested its will to become independent of the central authorities in Leopoldville. The situation
seemed very serious. War originating over the question of who
should possess and exploit the Katanga and its mineral riches,
a war into which the Soviet Union and the United States might
be drawn, seemed possible. The situation looked extremely
dangerous to close observers, especially since it developed less
than three months after the violent conclusion of the abortive
summit meeting in Paris and Khrushchev's and Malinowski's
threatening speeches. The general tension was increased, in addition, by a most unfortunate incident. On July 1st, 1960, an
American BR-47 reconnaisance airplane had been shot down by
Soviet pilots in the far north, near the Kola peninsula, over the
Barents Sea, and probably over international waters. The incident was unexpectedly exploited in a diplomatic move on July

11. In notes couched in the most violent terms the United States, the United Kingdom and Norway were attacked and threatened by the Soviet Union.

Secretary General Hammarskjöld expressed the prevailing deep apprehensions shared by many governments, when he said in the Security Council of the United Nations meeting on the crisis over the Katanga on August 8, 1960: "The solution of this problem is a question of peace and war. And when saying peace or war I do not limit my perspective to the Congo. . ."[9]

The immediate danger was averted by the courageous and skilful action of Dag Hammarskjöld, who went, accompanied by a Moroccan and an Indian General and two Swedish companies, to Elisabethville in the Katanga, to try to reach a direct understanding with the ruler of the province, Moise Tshombe. His attempt to secure a peaceful solution brought him into sharp opposition to Lumumba, who insisted on the total removal of the provincial authorities and their private and semi-private army by force, and wanted the UN force be placed under his own authority.

The Soviet Union still seemed to hope to be able to gain control in the Congo by supporting Lumumba, who by now was engaged in a confused fight with rivaling Congolese leaders. He received from Russia a few trucks and some aircraft in order to carry the elements of the *force publique* supporting him to the danger spots. In addition, Russian military and police instructors and personnel for technical help were channeled into the area. The conflict between Lumumba and Hammarskjöld was expanded by the Kremlin into a conflict between the Soviet Union and the United Nations.

In the struggle between the Congolese politicians the events soon took a dramatic turn, adverse to the Russian plans. Lumumba was dismissed by President Kasavubu on September 5. On September 11, a Sunday, Lumumba tried to seize, with a few soldiers, the radio station of Leopoldville. He was arrested, then freed again. The Chief of Staff, Colonel Joseph Mobutu, declared on September 13, that he had substituted the government by a

---

[9] *United Nations Yearbook* 1960 (New York, 1961), 55.

cabinet of experts, a Council of General Commissioners, protected by the army. On September 15, the Tass Agency announced in Moscow that Mobutu had been arrested. Actually, he was in full control and Lumumba in guarded residence, protected by UN troops. Lumumba later escaped, was brought to Katanga and on January 17, 1961, assassinated.

In the days during which these fights for dominance took place, the danger of great power action seemed imminent. While Moscow announced the arrest of Colonel Mobutu, the representative of the Soviet Union, Valerian Zorin, in a fiery speech in the Security Council, attacked the United Nations and the western powers for their alleged aggression. In reply, the delegate of the United States remarked that a unilateral action by the Soviet Union would necessarily provoke *another* unilateral action.

Such unilateral actions did not materialize. The following day, on September 16, 1960, the Soviet embassy in Leopoldville and its whole staff of advisors and experts were expelled by Colonel Mobutu. The United Nations forces, under the title *Operation des Nations Unies au Congo,* ONUC, expanded and consolidated their grip on the country. The Congolese parliament reconvened in June, 1961, and a government of national unity was formed on August 2, 1961. In spite of the severe crisis over the secession of Katanga in which Dag Hammarskjöld lost his life, in spite of the continuing tribal war, civil war, and government instability, the danger of the Congo becoming a source of general war was averted.

Whatever the significance of these later events and crises may have been for the international scene, the Soviet rulers had probably reached the conclusion as early as the first days of August of the fateful year of 1960 that the attempt to become the dominant influence in Africa, according to their preconceived doctrine, had failed.

The confrontation in which the Soviet Union under the leadership of Chairman Khrushchev had engaged, a confrontation within the framework of intervention, designed to force the United Nations to withdraw from the Congo and to take its place as the power eventually establishing peace and order and presiding over the reconstruction and exploitation of the country ended in defeat for the Soviets.

New York - the United Nations

Khrushchev, profoundly hurt by this outcome, at once opened a new confrontation. It was designed, this time, to destroy the United Nations which had proved to be such a powerful instrument of opposition to the Kremlin's ambitions and to humiliate the Western nations.

On June 27, 1960, the Ten Nations Disarmament Commission of the United Nations in Geneva had been broken up in a way most offensive to the Western powers. The Soviet delegate Zorin had made an abrupt declaration and walked out of the conference hall together with the delegates of four satellite countries. This incident was conveniently used as a starting point and pretext for transforming the forthcoming 15th General Assembly of the United Nations into a special forum in which Khrushchev hoped to achieve his aim. Moscow demanded that since the disarmament negotiations had failed in the Ten Nations Committee, they should be resumed by heads of governments themselves in the General Assembly. In August, in an article in *Pravda,* Khrushchev's intention to chair the Soviet Delegation in New York, was announced. The article added the suggestion that all delegations should be led by the heads of governments. The proposal was eagerly seized upon by ambitious men like Tito, Sukarno, Castro, Nehru, Nasser. The General Assembly convened, on September 20, 1960, in an ambiance of solemnity and expectation.

After President Eisenhower had addressed the gathering of heads of governments, Khrushchev made his first speech on September 23. He violently attacked the Secretary General of the United Nations, accusing him of illegal intervention in the Congo. After demanding Hammarskjöld's resignation, he went on to propose the abolition of the office of Secretary General. He proposed that, instead of a Secretary General, a committee of three should direct the United Nations. This committee would be composed of a representative of a communist country, a representative of a Western nation and one from the uncommitted nations, which, by not joining any alliance, pretended to keep aloof from the Cold War. The committee would have to be unanimous in taking its decisions, a step synonymous with the introduction of the Soviet veto in this body. The formula corresponded to the *troika* system, which the Soviet Union had tried to introduce in every international organization, commencing with the armistice commission set up by the conference of 1954 on Vietnam, then resumed in the negotiations on the inspection of a ban of nuclear testing in January, 1961, and later in the negotiations about Laos. Lest any one not see that the new proposals were meant to paralyze the United Nations, and to exclude the influence of the western nations, he was made fully aware of it by Khrushchev's suggestion that the headquarters of the UN be removed from New York and possibly transferred to the Soviet Union.

With this attempt to paralyze and possibly destroy the world organization, the Soviet dictator evidently had gone too far. He had antagonized the governments of many of the Asian and African states, to whom he constantly appealed in his attacks against the West, against colonialism and imperialism, hoping to win their support for the "grand design." Such support was not forthcoming, because the developing countries had found in the United Nations a forum where they could play a role which they otherwise would never have played; they also found there useful information and technical assistance. They basically approved the intervention in the Congo, in which their armed forces played a great role, and which had prevented the confrontation between the world powers from escalating into a war in which Africa might have been the main theater and the victim. They did not favor a basic change which would weaken their organization. And, finally, the Soviet speaker had made the mistake of putting Latin American nations in the same category as the former colonial peoples which had obtained their independence only recently. The Latin Americans, with their century-old proud tradition of freedom and independence and their great influence, often enhanced by the personal qualities of their representatives in the international bodies, could not be interested in the Russian plans.

That the whole procedure was planned as a confrontation of will power, resolve, and risk-taking was evidenced by Chairman Khrushchev's extraordinary personal behavior in the plenary meetings of the Assembly. His language was violent and sometimes unparliamentary. When Hammarskjöld after defending the office of Secretary General drew a long ovation from the Assembly, Khrushchev pounded his desk with his fist. When the representative of the Philippines tired of the continuous attacks against "colonialism" and pointed out on October 12 that the Soviet Union was also a colonial power and that the Eastern European peoples, deprived by Moscow of their freedom, should be included in the debate on the resolution demanding early independence of all nations still under any kind of foreign rule, Khrushchev performed his unprecedented and famous act. He took off one of his shoes, banged his desk with it, brandished it at the Philippine speaker, and tried to interrupt him by shouting insults. This undoubtedly reflected his boisterous temperament, yet it is hard to believe that it was a spontaneous action. It represented rather an attempt to humiliate the heads of government present, who had to witness such brutalities, and to impress on them the opinion that Russia's dictator was capable of irresponsible acts. Since he could unleash nuclear war at any time, it was expected that this would cause general fear. Fear, then, would induce governments to try not to irritate that dangerous man, not to provoke his wrath, and rather to yield to his demands. It was an attitude similar to that assumed five months earlier in the middle of the second Berlin confrontation, linked with the U-2 incident, and brought to its culmination in Paris.

Yet, these tactics of confrontation, with a show of reckless determination and violence on the one hand and a divided, bewildered and leaderless world of the nations trying to live in peace and normalcy on the other hand, did not bring the expected results.

Only a year later, when after the death on September 18, 1961, of Secretary General Hammarskjöld in an air crash in the Congo, the weakest possible candidate, the Burmese U Thant, was elected to be Secretary General, the Soviet Union came nearer to her aim. Thant was instructed to nominate as Under-secretaries a Russian and an American who would act as his deputies. This came close to the *troika* system, but since it did not include the veto power, it had not the nefarious effect which was originally intended.

Chapter IV

Confrontation In Our Time – Part Two

Berlin III - Vienna

Attention would soon revert to Berlin, where a new show of force, clad in new forms, was going to take place. As early as January 6, 1961, Khrushchev had said that he would "eradicate this splinter from the heart of Europe."[1] Yet, when the plan developed to meet President John F. Kennedy in Vienna early in June, the final confrontation was delayed.

The newly elected President of the United States and the Chairman of the Council of Ministers of the Soviet Union met in Vienna on June 3 and 4, 1961. The main object of President Kennedy was personally to get acquainted with his main opponent and to eliminate any danger of miscalculation in their common relationship. He was obsessed by the fear that one or the other side could underestimate the resolve of the other, and thereby precipitate an armed clash, which would have been avoided had the other known the opponent's resolve. Kennedy was obviously thinking in terms of the lessons of 1914 and 1939, where such miscalculation had played a sinister role. What Kennedy and his advisers ignored was that in accepting Vienna as the meeting place, he had made a gesture which in Russian eyes was a concession and a sign of weakness. The Russians regarded Vienna as a kind of ante-room to Moscow, and later presented the meeting there in such a way as to create the impression that young Kennedy had gone out of his way to be received by the elder statesman on the latter's territory and to pay his respects to him.

---

[1] Theodore C. Sorensen, *Kennedy* (London, 1965), 584.

The conversations between the two men touched on all problems of international policy. It was evident, however, that Khrushchev was mainly interested in Berlin, and that he tried to shake the American resolve to defend the freedom of West Berlin. This question was tackled on the second day of the conversations. Khrushchev took the offensive and stated that no force of the world could stop the Soviet Union from signing a peace treaty with the German Democratic Republic (DDR) and that it would be signed in December. However, a face-saving interim agreement to cover the next six months could be considered. The treaty would cancel all existing commitments, including the right of occupation and rights of access. It would end the state of war and establish a free city of West Berlin. Agreement on access would have to be negotiated in the future with the DDR. Under certain conditions Western troops would be tolerated in West Berlin, together with Soviet troops. If the West insisted on occupation rights after the treaty and if the borders of the DDR were violated, force would be met by force.[2]

Kennedy patiently stated the reasons why the United States could not abandon Berlin and her commitments towards its population, and why he had no intention to give up the rights of the Allies. He maintained that denying the West its contractual rights would be a belligerent act. The conversation eventually took a harsh and grim turn, and the words peace and war recurred frequently. At the end of the talks an official Soviet *aide memoire* was handed to Kennedy on Berlin and the test ban.

Kennedy went away from the conversation deeply disturbed. As Arthur Schlesinger reports, "He himself had indicated flexibility and admitted error, but Khrushchev had remained unmoved and unmovable."[3] The meeting with the President had visibly confirmed for Khrushchev his pre-conceived idea that he was dealing with a young, unexperienced and probably weak man, and that he could confidently go ahead with his plans.

---

[2] Arthur M. Schlesinger Jr., *A Thousand Days, John F. Kennedy in the White House* (London, 1965), 337.

[3] *ibid.*, 339.

Back in Moscow, Khrushchev issued a new ultimatum on the basis of his *aide memoire* which said that he would sign the peace treaty in December. He announced that the Soviet Union would increase defense expenditure by more than 30 percent. Tensions rose as threats met with manifestations of resolve. One of the consequences was that the stream of refugees, which had for a long time drained the zone in the middle and east of Germany occupied by the Soviet armies from its most active and best educated people, increased in a menacing way. Since the demarcation line had been closed long ago by the DDR, this stream was channeled through Berlin, where it was easy to go from the Eastern sector to one of the Western sectors. In August it was estimated that 3.5 million people, out of a population of 17 million of the DDR, had left and found refuge in the Federal Republic of Germany.

It was now necessary for Washington to reply to the Soviet *aide memoire*. It took the American diplomacy several weeks to draft the corresponding document, which reiterated the well known legal points involved in the confrontation. President Kennedy, however, wanted to give a clearer answer and did so in a televised speech on July 25, 1961. He explained to the American people that he would not allow the Communists to drive the Western powers out of Berlin, either gradually or by force. To underline this resolve, $3.25 billion were to be added to the defense budget. But force was to be combined with the willingness to negotiate. Kennedy added:

> To sum up: We seek peace, but we shall not surrender. That is the central meaning of this crisis, and the meaning of your government's policy.
>
> We will at all times be ready to talk, if talk will help. But we must also be ready to resist with force, if force is used upon us. Either alone would fail. Together they can serve the cause of freedom and peace.[4]

The typical elements of the confrontation now came to the fore: Political maneuver, diplomacy and negotiation had to be combined with a show of force and actual deployment of power in order to prevail.

---

[4] *Documents on American Foreign Policy* 1961 (New York: Council on Foreign Relations, 1962), 95.

Khrushchev answered the speech on August 7 in a similar vein. The fronts now seemed equally solid and impenetrable, the opponents stood *adversis frontibus,* no decision in view, no honorable and acceptable way out visible for either side. The strategic situation was clearly different from that which existed in the 1948/49 confrontation. At that time President Eisenhower had made it very clear that, in view of the weakness of their conventional forces on the spot, the United States and her allies did not think of proceding by force against the closing of the access roads to Berlin. In the event of an attack against their garrisons, larger operations on the ground and sustained resistance were not considered possible. He hinted, however, that massive retaliation was an eventuality.

In 1961, in a completely changed strategic environment, in which both sides had nuclear weapons and the corresponding delivery systems, President Kennedy expressed, by a systematic build-up of conventional forces in Europe and reserve forces in the United States, that force would be met with force on the spot. If such a showdown did not suffice to bring the opponent to the negotiating table, then nuclear force would be applied.

Berlin IV - The Wall and Nuclear Tests

In this situation the Soviets seemed immovable except by use of force, a circumstance which both sides wanted to avoid. The Soviets found the way out with a maneuver which, in retrospect, must be described as a stroke of genius. Was it Walter Ulbricht, the Chairman of the Council of State of the DDR, was it Khrushchev, or was it one of his advisers who found the solution? Was it the loose talk going on all the time in the West? In discussing the confrontation and the contractual rights which the West was bound to defend in West Berlin, on the *Autobahn* and the air corridors, it was repeatedly stated that the West, of course, could and would not interfere with what went on within the Soviet zone of occupation and within East Berlin. When the East showed its concern about the drainage of manpower and intellect by the stream of refugees through Berlin, many people shrugged their shoulders and remarked that it was the other side's problem to stop the movement. The Germans themselves were deeply concerned by the migration; they feared that gradually the area occupied by the Soviet army might be drained of the German population which then would be replaced by Slavic immigrants from the East; they wished it would cease. On July 30, Senator J. William Fulbright went on record in a televised interview saying: "I don't understand why the East Germans don't close their border because I think they have a right to close it."[5]

In the early morning of August 13, 1961, the demarcation line dividing East and West Berlin was closed by the *Volks-polizei*. Traffic across the line was practically halted and limited to a few checkpoints, where it was closely inspected and screened. This was the measure everybody had suggested, openly or tacitly, and which nobody, not even the contingency planners who had brooded over the Berlin question for months, had expected. The West was taken by surprise and, after voicing some weak protests, acquiesced.

In typical fashion, the second step of the Communists was taken a few days later. It consisted of building "the wall" all along the demarcation line, well within the Soviet Sector, yet for everyone to see. It was designed to block completely the way out for any would-be refugees and to make the already existing and effective police measures absolutely water-tight. Even more important, the ugly contrivance was to humiliate the West by demonstrating absolute recklessness and resolve in a way to which no corresponding answer could be found.

The sight of the wall was humiliating. After 1948 the area of Soviet occupation had been mentally excluded from Western responsibility and there was no point in trying to prevent the wall from being built, and no agreement among the Allies could have been reached on it. It simply was not part of the confrontation. Yet, to tolerate the sight of the concrete structure, capped with barbed wire, and to tolerate the human suffering which it created, were the equivalent of a defeat for the West. This was clearly understood in Germany and in the rest of Europe, perhaps less in the United States.

---

[5] Arthur M. Schlesinger Jr., *op. cit.,* 356.

For the first time, Khrushchev had scored a point in the contest of resolve, and an important one. Trust between the Allies and between the Germans and the Allies was undermined and never completely restored. The outcome was deep frustration, not because the Western powers could be accused of not having lived up to their commitments, and not because they had not acted, but because nobody could possibly say what they should have done within the commitments and what would have been right.

The curtain had dropped on the second act of this particular confrontation. The West was humiliated and divided. Yet, by the very nature of the instrument which Khrushchev had used to achieve this, he had blocked his own way to go any further. The *status quo,* which he had sought to change, seemed now more immovable than ever. In addition, the sense of urgency had gone out of the desire to eliminate the allied presence in Berlin; the deadly loss of DDR blood, the stream of refugees had been stopped.

Khrushchev therefore reverted to his old plan to sign a peace treaty with the DDR at the end of the year, and then to seal off the access to Berlin and demand the withdrawal of the Allied occupation forces. This, however, could only be effective when backed by an overwhelming military threat. Such threats promised to be effective. The pacifist movement in England and similar movements, which ran under such slogans as "ban the bomb," or "better red than dead" had only to be encouraged by creating anguish to a point where they would paralyze the governments and force them to yield to pressure.

The earlier disarmament talks provided the lever. On October 31, 1958, a three power conference had met in Geneva, with instructions to find a way to discontinue the testing of nuclear weapons. To improve the atmosphere for the talks, General Eisenhower had suggested on August 22, 1958 that the tests be interrupted informally at the date of the beginning of the conference. This proposal was violently rejected by the Soviets, and they accompanied the opening sessions in Geneva on November 1st and 3rd, 1958 with heavy explosions in the Southern Soviet Union.

The United States, however, stuck to its offer and refrained from holding nuclear tests. On August 26, 1959, the American government announced that it would not conduct any tests until the end of the year. The following day the British government announced that they would not test any nuclear device as long as useful negotiations were proceeding in Geneva. The next day the Soviet Union declared it would not resume testing as long as the Western powers did not.[6]

In the meantime, the Berlin confrontation had come to a relatively successful conclusion, for the Soviets, but had not reached the anticipated results. It had to be reopened. On August 30, 1961, the Soviet Union declared publicly, that she would resume testing. It is thought that the decision had been reached as early as March, on technological and strategic as well as on political grounds. Yet it is significant that the decision was not announced until immediately after the successful conclusion of the second act of the Berlin confrontation.[7]

The belief that the nuclear explosions were nothing less than a new move in the Berlin confrontation was confirmed by the Soviet statement of August 30. It said among other things:

> A new demonstration of strength in response to the Soviet proposals concerning the German peace treaty is the dispatch to West Berlin of additional troops and armaments by the United States and Britain. . . The Soviet Government would not have fulfilled its sacred duty to the peoples of its country, to the peoples of the socialist countries and to all peoples striving for peaceful life if in the face of threats and military preparations that seized the United States and some other NATO countries it had not used the available possibilities for perfecting the most effective types of weapons that can cool the hotheads in the capitals of some NATO powers.
> The Soviet Union has worked out designs for creating a series of superpowerful nuclear bombs of 20, 30, 50 and 100 million tons of TNT; and powerful rockets, similar to those with the help of which Major Y. A. Gagarin and Major G. S. Titov made their unequalled cosmic flights around the earth, can lift and deliver such nuclear bombs to any point of the globe wherefrom an attack on the Soviet Union or other socialist countries could be launched.[8]

---

[6] "Geneva Conference on the Discontinuance of Nuclear Weapons Tests." *US Disarmament Administration, Department of State* (Washington, 1961), 375.

[7] David E. Mark, *Die Einstellung der Kernwaffenversuche* (Frankfurt/M., 1965), 87.

[8] "Geneva Conference on the Discontinuance of Nuclear Weapons Tests." *loc. cit.,* 616.

The White House replied with a short statement, saying:

What the Soviet Union is obviously testing is not only nuclear devices but the will and the determination of the free world to resist such tactics and to defend freedom.[9]

On September 5 Washington added that resumption of nuclear tests had been ordered, in the laboratory and underground, but with no fallout.

The day after Moscow had announced the decision to break the pledge of 1959, and had stated its new determination to force the West to accept the signing of the peace treaty with the DDR and to give up its rights in Berlin, the atomic mushrooms and the fireballs of gigantic nuclear explosions appeared in the far north of the Soviet Union; radioactivity in the atmosphere of the whole of the Northern hemisphere increased dramatically. The series of about fifty explosions culminated on October 30 in one which proved to be more than 50 megatons, and which western scientists estimated to equal 100 megatons.

This show of force, unprecedented in any of the confrontations which had so far tested the Western world's resolve, almost a kind of limited nuclear war, was accompanied by the corresponding moves designed to harvest the political result of the confrontation. At the 22nd Congress of the Communist Party of the Soviet Union, Khrushchev once more withdrew the ultimatum. He declared he would not insist on signing the peace treaty with the DDR before the end of the year, on condition that the West showed a readiness to solve the German problem.

The West, however, did not walk into the trap. No negotiations were resumed, since nothing seemed negotiable under the circumstances. On March 2, 1962, Kennedy made the announcement—after having secured a half-hearted agreement from the British Prime Minister Macmillan who had not spared any effort to delay or prevent a decision—that the United States would resume atmospheric testing. On April 25 the tests began over Christmas Island in the Central Pacific. The Soviet move, by that decision, seemed neutralized, and Khrushchev had to look for a new approach by which to attack the fortress Berlin.

---

[9] *ibid.*, 620.

Cuba 1962

The Soviet dictator had by now, one may safely assume, come to the conclusion that his nuclear threats, mainly directed against Europe, were not strong enough to shake the United States' resolve to stand firm on Berlin. The fate of the European peoples which the Soviets held as hostages under the threat of nuclear annihilation, did not seem to be an argument strong enough to move the Americans. The basis of this judgement was the fact that the United States still retained a great advantage in intercontinental delivery of nuclear warheads, whereas the Soviet Union was in a state of decisive superiority in the area which she could reach with the medium range ballistic missiles and her medium bombers.

Early in 1962 the relationship of strategic forces was roughly the following:

United States

ICBM	120
IRBM, MRBM	200
Intercontinental bombers	600
Medium range bombers	1,600

Soviet Union

ICBM	70
IRBM, MRBM	700
Intercontinental bombers	190
Medium range bombers	1,400

The number of ICBMs in the United States' arsenal was scheduled to increase at a rapid rate, because the solid-fueled *Minuteman* system on hardened bases was to be deployed in the near future.

The Soviet's problem then was how rapidly to improve the relationship in the intercontinental field, in order be able to threaten the United States itself instead of its allies in Europe. The step which Khrushchev took in order to optimize this relationship led to the most dramatic confrontation of our time, the Cuban missile crisis.

From the day Dr. Fidel Castro had seized power in Havana on January 6, 1959, the relationship between Cuba and the United States of America had deteriorated. Gradually Moscow came to replace the formerly dominating American influence on the sugar island. Agriculture, industry, the infrastructure were helped in their development by increasing numbers of experts sent from the Soviet Union and other communist countries.

While Castro was actually, though not effectively, threatened by Cuban refugees, who prepared in the neighboring countries a military overthrow of his regime, it was most unlikely that the government of the United States would reach a decision to intervene by force against communist domination on the island. The attempted invasion of April 17, 1961, at the Bay of Pigs, by Cuban refugees, while abetted and supported by the United States, gives ample proof of how reluctant the great neighbor in the North was to come to grips with the unpleasant yet tolerable situation in Cuba. However, the Castro regime felt threatened. One has to remember that its fears, though, were not entirely products of heated imagination; the U.S. Navy had scheduled for 1962 an amphibious exercise *Philbriglex-62* the purpose of which was the overthrow of a mythical dictator named "Ortsac." Cuba relied more and more on Soviet support to improve its defenses by the introduction of modern arms, including anti-aircraft missiles from Russia and the training of the Cuban army by Soviet instructors. The foothold which the Soviets gradually and probably to their own surprise, had thus gained in the Western hemisphere became the basis of a new phase of the Berlin confrontation, which Khrushchev decided to open.

The plan today seems simple enough. The massive threat against the peoples of Europe had not been effective—according to Soviet opinion the "governing circles" and "Wall Street" felt safe enough and protected by their superior strength in intercontinental missiles and by the distance separating them from the Soviet Union—and it was essential to be able to threaten the Americans in the very heart of their power. The period of the American election campaign in 1962—July to November—could be used conveniently to transfer a number of MRBMs, IRBMs and medium range bombers to bases in Cuba. These could be installed there under the relatively safe protection of military personnel which was already there and which could be reinforced. Cuban acquiescence could easily be secured, since such powerful weaponry would be thought by the Cubans to enhance the prestige of the regime,[10] might improve their domestic situation and the bargaining position vis-a-vis the United States. Some passionate revolutionaries and haters of North America like Che Guevara may even have dreamed, in Chinese fashion, of dealing with the Russian weapons, a devastating blow to the arch-enemy. If the Americans discovered the build-up, which in view of the closeness and the constant movement of intelligence agents between the two countries seemed likely, they would not, according to the Soviet text books, be able to react during an election campaign—even an off-term election. One of the shibboleths of "scientific" Marxist-Leninist-Stalinist thinking takes it for granted that a democracy like the American democracy is paralyzed during pre-election time. How much Khrushchev relied on this aspect is reflected in a message which he channeled through the Soviet ambassador Dobrinin and President Kennedy's adviser Sorensen to the president. According to Sorensen's notes it read:

> Nothing will be undertaken before the American Congressional elections that could complicate the internal situation or aggravate the tension in the relations between our two countries. . . provided there are no actions taken on the other side which would change the situation. This includes a German peace settlement and West Berlin. . .[11]

Therefore the military build-up in Cuba was performed with extraordinary speed. By mid-October, 1962, 24 launch pads for 48 MRBMs were being installed, and between 24 and 32 IRBMs were under way to Cuba. Their launching pads were under construction. Forty-two Il-28 medium bombers, according to Soviet sources, were being uncrated and assembled on Cuban air bases.

This force would have redressed the imbalance of strategic forces existing in the direct relationship between the Soviet

---

[10] Albert and Roberta Wohlstetter, *Controlling the Risks in Cuba*, Adelphi Paper No. 17 (London, 1965), 4.

[11] Theodore Sorensen, *op. cit.*, 667.

Union and the United States. The IRBMs and the Il-28 bombers were able to cover the whole of the continental United States, except the North East, with little or no warning, since their threat came from a direction where it could not be detected by the then existing American ballistic missile early warning system installed in the North and East. The MRBMs were capable of reaching important centers and installations in the Southern States, especially vital bases of the Strategic Air Command. Add 80 units to the 70 Soviet ICBMs listed in the table on page 58, and the figure of 150 missiles able to reach the continental United States clearly outruns the 120 American ICBMs then operative and able to threaten the Soviet Union.

Based on such an improved power relationship, the Soviet dictator could hope to resume the confrontation over Berlin, after November 6, the new deadline he had set. Everything indicated that he was planning to appear, as he had done in 1960, at the General Assembly of the United Nations. There, carried by the waves of anti-Americanism he would arouse in the delegates, he hoped to bring about a summit meeting and separate the United States from its allies. He would see whether the American President, under the pressure of a gullible public opinion, which might have been willing to risk nuclear war on the back of the European peoples, would continue to stand firm on Berlin when he could threaten the Americans directly. No American man or woman in his or her senses, so the men in the Kremlin thought, would be willing to trade New York and Washington for Berlin.

Such was the basis for the third act of the Berlin confrontation, and Khrushchev may have felt confident—probably more confident than his own military advisers—that this time he would score a point.

This third act of the Berlin confrontation, which would have had a thermonuclear character, as did the preceding one when nuclear testing was employed as the ultima ratio, never took place. It was forestalled by a confrontation over Cuba; Khrushchev suffered a defeat from which he never recovered and which finally contributed to his fall on October 15, 1964.

The Soviet military build-up on Cuba was closely watched by the administration in Washington as early as mid-summer, when a daily special intelligence report to the White House on Cuba began. By mid-October the build-up had reached proportions and characteristics which seemed important enough to affect the strategic balance and to warrant action. On October 15, 1962, the aerial photographs taken by the U-2 reconnaissance planes over Western Cuba brought tangible proof that a base for 16 to 24 Medium Range Ballistic Missiles was being built. Construction seemed to have reached a point where the missiles could be operative around the 1st of November.[12] The American President, assisted by a special group of advisers, later called the Executive Committee of the National Security Council, acted with great circumspection and speed.

The development of the crisis and confrontation, its culmination and ebbing away have been described in great detail in the extensive literature it has stimulated,[13] and it is not necessary to retrace it here. We shall limit ourselves, therefore, to the interpretation of the character of the crisis as one of the most significant confrontations of our time.

Many interpretations have since been given to the motivations of the Kremlin and to what might have come out of the move had it succeeded. Hence, it is not surprising that the men in the White House, confronted with the facts, considered and weighed many interpretations and possibilities of reacting. The interpretations ranged from explaining the move as an effort to consolidate the Castro regime and to make it safe against an intervention by the United States on the one hand, to explaining it as an attempt to tip the total strategic balance, on the other. Among the recommendations made there could be discern-

---

[12] Wohlstetter, *op. cit.*, 12.

[13] Among the best presentations of facts and their interpretation one may cite:

Claude Delmas, *Histoire politique de la bombe atomique* (Paris, 1967), 263 ff.; "Cuba Missile Confrontation," from *The New York Times*, November 6, 1962; *Survival*, Vol. 5, No. 1, January/February, 1963 (London: Institute for Strategic Studies, 1963); Louis J. Halle, *op. cit.*, 406 ff.; Robert F. Kennedy, *13 Days, The Cuban Missile Crisis 1962* (London, 1969); David L. Larson, ed., *The Cuban Crisis of 1962, Selected Documents and Chronology* (Boston, 1963); Henry M. Pachter, *Collision Course: The Cuban Missile Crisis and Coexistence* (London, 1963); Arthur M. Schlesinger *op. cit.*, 680 ff.; Theodore Sorensen, op. cit., 667 ff.; Wohlstetter, *op. cit.*

ed at the bottom of the ladder those of the advocates of a simple diplomatic protest, on the top rungs the recommendation to destroy the bases by aerial bombardment or even to occupy Cuba.

It is well known that President Kennedy interpreted the situation above all as one pertaining to the Cold War, a move designed to shatter the United State's prestige and position and to force it to retreat from Berlin. He made this clear when he said, on October 22, 1962, in his televised address to the American people, which was his opening move of the confrontation:

> We no longer live in a world where only the actual firing of weapons represents a sufficient challenge to a nation's security to constitute maximum peril. Nuclear weapons are so destructive and ballistic missiles are so swift, that any substantially increased possibility of their use or any sudden change in their deployment may well be regarded as a definite threat to peace.[14]

The object of the next steps to be taken was to prevent such a change in the deployment of nuclear weapons and to avoid a tipping of the existing balance in favor of the Soviet Union. From the very beginning it never occurred to any planner in Washington that the reply could or should be nuclear. As the Secretary of Defense, Robert McNamara later wrote: 'He understood then as now that above all else a U.S. President must, while defending our vital interests, prevent the confrontation between nuclear powers which can lead to nuclear holocaust.'[15]

Gradually the idea of a limited blockade of Cuba, to be called "quarantine," emerged from the studies and discussions as a possible solution. The plan was to communicate to the Soviet Union that, whereas other shipping would not be interfered with, no ships carrying offensive weapons would be allowed to approach the island, and that she was expected to remove the missiles and bombers from the Caribbean area. This had the advantage, considered essential, that blockade necessitated only a limited deployment of force, which could gradually be increased if it proved necessary. On the other hand, the move

---

[14] *Documents on American Foreign Relations 1962* (New York: Council on Foreign Relations, 1963), 376.

[15] Robert F. Kennedy, *op. cit.,* McNamara in the Preface, 21.

left the Soviets space to maneuver and to extricate themselves from the confrontation in a way which would not appear as a humiliating retreat.

The United States was in a favorable position to build up its forces in the area for all possible contingencies, including naval action against Soviet ships and their eventual escorts trying to ignore the quarantine, or air strikes and troop landings against the bases in Cuba and the Soviet personnel stationed there in the event Moscow chose not to remove the missiles and the servicing personnel. The Soviets, in a position of absolute inferiority in the area, could choose between accepting defeat in a local armed clash or taking diversionary action, for example against Berlin or Turkey, or threatening a nuclear strike against the United States, or backing down.

The proclamation of the President issued on October 24, announcing the interdiction of delivery of offensive weapons to Cuba, and the orders subsequently given to the naval command, made it clear that the quarantine would be selective and handled with utmost care and restraint. Force would be used only to the extent necessary, only in self-defense or in case of failure or refusal to comply with directions.

Those who objected to the idea of blockade or quarantine argued that an intervention in Cuba against the missile sites would amount to a conflict with Cuba, whereas stopping the Soviet ships, and perhaps searching them, would, in case they were escorted by warships, inevitably lead to a naval confrontation with the Soviets. The ships were actually escorted, as it transpired on the 24th, by Soviet submarines.

The naval confrontation, however, did not develop. On October 24, sixteen of the eighteen ships heading toward Cuba had stopped. The Soviet tanker *Bucharest,* which continued on her course, was hailed and, after identifying itself, let through the barrier. The same happened with a passenger ship from the DDR. On October 26, the Soviet ships began to return towards their points of departure.

The military confrontation, however, continued to build up. Work on the missile sites went on at an accelerated pace. The United States had concentrated several divisions in Florida, with the corresponding landing craft and airlift and were ready for an invasion of Cuba. The Air Force made low-level flights over the critical areas. One U-2 was shot down over Cuba by the Russians. At the United Nations, where the Security Council had met at the request of the United States, a diplomatic and rhetorical phase of the confrontation rolled on.

When they gave orders to the ships to stop and to return, the Soviets evidently abandoned the plan to bring strategic weapons to Cuba, but what did they intend to do with the equipment which was already landed and which was being readied for firing?

On Friday, October 26, the first signals were received that Khrushchev was looking for a way out of the intolerable situation. On Friday night a message from Moscow reached Washington; it was almost simultaneously broadcast, and it was to the effect that the necessity for the Soviet presence in Cuba would disappear if the United States would give assurance that it would not invade Cuba and if it would lift the quarantine. On the following morning a second letter was broadcast by Radio Moscow to introduce a new condition. It proposed that the United States should remove its *Jupiter* missiles from Turkey in exchange for a non-aggression pledge by Moscow to Ankara, and that the Soviet Union would remove its missiles from Cuba in exchange for a non-aggression pledge by the United States to Cuba. Following a proposal by Robert Kennedy, this second letter was ignored; the offer of the first letter was accepted under the condition that the offensive weapons be made inoperable under United Nations supervision.

On Sunday, October 28, Khrushchev replied, indicating that work on the missiles sites would stop and that the missiles would be sent back to the Soviet Union. The confrontation was over and had ended again with defeat for the Soviet dictator. The *Jupiter* missiles, already obsolescent when the NATO defense ministers, in March 1958, had reached agreement in principle on their deployment, were quietly removed in 1963 from their foreign bases. It had been deemed dangerous to include them instantly in a settlement of the Cuban confrontation; the outcome of it might have been blurred by this concession, however marginal it was.

The Cuban missile crisis was generally interpreted as a thermonuclear confrontation, since it concerned the installation of nuclear missiles on the Island of Cuba. However, this was not the case.[16] The United States made no statement to the effect that they would use nuclear weapons against missile sites, and they hinted even less that they would use nuclear retaliation against the Soviet Union in the event the build-up on Cuba continued. The pressure on the Soviets originated from the preparations for an invasion of Cuba by conventional forces, and from the fear that vessels carrying precious equipment might be sunk or seized by the U.S. Navy. In this phase prior to the missiles becoming operative, the Soviet military threat consisted of the possibility that warships enforcing the quarantine could be attacked and sunk by Soviet submarines operating in the area, or by Soviet fighter-bombers stationed in Cuba. No direct nuclear threat such as on earlier occasions was made. It was a confrontation of conventional forces,[17] and the decision was brought about by the inferiority of Soviet conventional power in the threater of conflict.

The possibility existed, of course, and it was carefully considered that Khrushchev might add new elements to the confrontation in the Caribbean Sea. He might have introduced new demands on Berlin, or reiterated the old ones, or, in relation to the American missile bases in Turkey and Italy, he might have asked as he actually did at one moment, for concessions there as part of a settlement over the missiles in Cuba. He might even have taken local action in such remote areas, which then could have precipitated a nuclear confrontation—as seemed likely if the theater of diversion was to be Berlin. However, such extension of the conflict did not occur because of the existing nuclear balance between the United States and the Soviet Union. This balance was—and still is—a lasting feature, and therefore no specific part of the Cuban confrontation.

---

[16] Herman Kahn, *On Escalation, Metaphors and Scenarios* (New York, 1965), 249.

[17] Urs Schwarz, *American Strategy: A New Perspective* (New York, 1966). 154.

Confrontation in Asia

Years later, when it lost a confrontation because of conventional military inferiority on the spot, the United States was to find itself in the same humiliating position as the Soviet Union at the end of the Cuban incident. The occasion was the *Pueblo* incident.

On January 23, 1968, the U.S. naval vessel *Pueblo* was on a routine mission in the Sea of Japan, off the coast of North Korea. The *Pueblo* was unarmed but carried sophisticated electronic equipment designed to monitor the signals exchanged between North Korean forces and also between Soviet forces in and around Vladivostok, and perhaps to intercept messages in the air far inside China and the Soviet Union. North Korean patrol boats approached the *Pueblo,* their crews boarded the ship in a surprise action, preventing the destruction of the secret equipment and secret codes and documents aboard. The captain was forced to take course to the North Korean port of Wonsan, where he and his crew were made prisoners.

It was a short and swift confrontation between little North Korea and the giant United States. Since the radio ship was not protected by air or naval forces, as would have seemed mandatory for such a dangerous mission, the United States found itself in a most difficult position. Should the Navy descend on the North Koreans in a Nelsonian action and free the captive ship? This would have meant almost certain death for the crew of 93 in Korean captivity, and the corresponding almost irresistible compulsion to retaliate—which would have meant war on North Korea. Such a war woud have precipitated a major conflict with China and probably also with the Soviet Union, especially since it seemed likely that the Koreans had acted under Soviet instructions. It looked as if the United States was confronting the Soviet Union by proxy.

No countermeasures which did not imply serious risk of war and perhaps escalation of war to a much bigger conflict could be discovered—no blockade this time, no allies willing to share the burden, no effective local threat. President Lyndon B. Johnson, deeply involved in the war in Vietnam and its unfortunate consequences on the domestic scene, could absolutely not afford to have the confrontation degenerate into a major conflict. His administration had, therefore, to engage in protracted negotiations about the fate of the crew, which had to be saved at almost any cost. The contest ended in a compromise: The United States had to present humiliating apologies, and this permitted the North Koreans to extricate themselves from the confrontation—which was not altogether reassuring for them—by setting the prisoners free.

East Asia has been, ever since the end of World War II, the theater of armed conflict, subversion, intervention and confrontation. The protagonists of the main confrontations are or were the People's Republic of China, the Soviet Union, India, Indonesia, and the United States.

A situation which immediately comes to the mind, the antagonism existing between the Chinese government in Peking and the government in Taipeh on Formosa, the self-styled Republic of China, is difficult to construe as a true confrontation. It is rather a continued civil war. It ended, as far as the Chinese mainland is concerned, in 1949 by the establishment of communist domination over all of China, yet continued when what remained of the Kuomintang government and its armies sought and found refuge on the island of Taiwan.

Confrontation, however, existed between Peking and the United States. Ever since President Truman, in a side-move originating from the conflict in Korea, ordered the Seventh Fleet in 1950 to separate the two Chinese civil war antagonists in the Straits of Formosa, and especially since Washington concluded, on December 2, 1954, a security arrangement with Taipeh, in which it assumed an obligation of defending the island of Formosa and the Pescadores Islands in the Straits of Formosa, the United States has been engaged in maneuvers designed to prevent military action across the straits. In January 1955 a joint resolution of the two houses of Congress authorized the President to use military force in defense of Formosa and the Pescadores. This resolution, which in a strictly constitutional sense was not needed, was designed as a powerful signal to Peking and was perfectly well understood.

Significantly, the military operations did not directly involve the two great antagonists—China and the United States—in a sense that their armed forces did meet face to face. They consisted mainly of an exchange of artillery fire between the batteries of the People's Liberation Army installed on the Chinese mainland and the heavy guns of the Nationalists installed on the off-shore island of Quemoy and Matsu, situated near the approaches of the ports of Amoy and Foochow. These islands were *not* expressly included in the American guarantee, and yet their fate would have greatly influenced the outcome of the confrontation. The group of the Pescadores, an attack on which would have resulted almost automatically in an intervention by the U.S. Seventh Fleet, were left alone.

Parallel to this mutual show of force and directed at objectives others than those on which the basic conflict turned were the formal Sino-American conferences inaugurated on an ambassadorial level. These began in Geneva and were later transferred to Warsaw, where they took place over many years and are still continuing.

It is interesting to note that the Chinese display of force along the south coast in the summer of 1958 coincided with the deepening of the conflict between Peking and Moscow, which had begun in November 1957, at the conference of twelve ruling Communist parties in Moscow. Mao Tse-tung took part in that conference, and we now know that Khrushchev, during his late visit to Peking from July 31 through August 3, 1958, was formally asked to support the display of military force against the islands of Quemoi and Matsu. Khrushchev refused. Peking's aim had evidently been to draw the Soviet Union into its confrontation with the United States and to put a stop to the dreaded *rapprochement* between Moscow and Washington. Khrushchev's refusal to be maneuvered away from his main interest, which then lay in Berlin and Western Europe, was answered by the Chinese in mid-August by an increase of the artillery fire, against the islands. India's offer to assume the role of a mediator in the off-shore conflict—designed to help its great protector, Moscow—was rejected with disdain by Peking. The effort directed against the off-shore islands was designed to show China's resolve in the fight against imperialism, in contrast to the Soviet's weak "revisionist" policy. The operation was not successful. It did not yield any military results—which it was actually not designed to achieve—and it did not reverse the course of the Kremlin's policy. Gradually the confrontation petered out and after a few years was practically forgotten.

Thus the culmination of the confrontation in 1958 is an example of how a situation of basic conflict between two antagonists, China and the United States, could be manipulated so as to become an instrument in the manipulation of a much more important confrontation then developing, the confrontation between two rival sources of Marxism-Leninism and, at the same time, between the capitals of two rival governments of nationalist and imperialist great powers.

In March, 1959, the Tibetans rose against the fast progressing infiltration of Chinese power into the country and the growing Chinese influence over it. Peking seized the occasion and occupied the whole of Tibet, establishing complete political control over the country. The stage was now set for a decisive confrontation between China and her rival in Asia, India.

Ever increasing claims on border areas in the Himalayas, which acccording to the existing maps belonged to India or to the intermediary border states of Bhutan, Sikkim and Nepal, were made by Peking. In the end these claims amounted to more than 100,000 square kilometers. Airfields were built in Tibet; a network of strategic roads leading up to the Himalayan passes was started and a railroad linking Lanchow and Sinking with Lhasa was begun. In the winter of 1959/60 the first clashes of arms occurred in the border region with India. The object, of course, was not to conquer the territory, but to inflict a defeat on India and, in the same process, on Soviet prestige. India's economy was to be weakened in order to prove the superiority of the Chinese communist system for a developing country over the rather liberal socialist and democratic methods applied by India. The possibility of India's giving economic and technological aid in Asia and Africa and thereby gaining influence as the leading uncommitted, unaligned nation was to be undermined. The creation of an intermediary area between what the Chinese called imperialism on the one hand and socialism on the other hand, an area within which Moscow was successfully attempting to create close economic and political links, was to be prevented.

The operation was thus far successful. From then on, India had to devote a much higher percentage of its resources to national defense than before, and the prestige of the Nehru government was generally weakened, at home and abroad.

Pressure was increased in the fall of 1962. In October, the People's Liberation Army attacked simultaneously the North East Frontier Agency in the area of the northen tributaries of the Brahmaputra, and far to the West, in Ladakh, in the East of Kashmir. Indian resistance collapsed in the North East, whereas in Ladakh opposition to the aggression was more successful. China did not press her military success, which would have been easy because India was militarily unprepared; she had concentrated most of her limited forces against Pakistan. On the contrary, as early as November, Peking announced unilateral withdrawal of troops from the North East Frontier Agency's territory and offered an arrangement in Ladakh, including a demilitarized zone.

This shows that in spite of armed clashes involved, the operation was far from being planned as a war, even a limited war. It was a typical confrontation, successfully conducted by China. India's military inferiority was made visible to the developing world. The Soviet Union and the Western powers were compelled to increase their military assistance to India, causing deep distrust in Pakistan and forcing its government to approach China as its protector. India was induced to divert more of its scarce means from developing its economy to defense. Thus India's defense budget rose from roughly 4 billion rupees to 9 billion rupees in 1963-64.

The subsequent outbreaks of armed violence on the India-Pakistan border in 1965, first in the Rann of Kutch and later more generally as a war in the Punjab and Kashmir, were influenced by situations created as the result of the confrontation between China and India. They were, however, acts of war in a traditional sense, and were accordingly settled by an armistice.

The second conflict was fully terminated on January 10, 1966, by an agreement signed in Tashkent with the Russians acting as mediators, and the first was settled by arbitration within the framework of the United Nations on July 4, 1969.

South East Asia

A spectacular confrontation developed between the Netherlands and Indonesia in the early sixties over the future of the Western half of New Guinea, or West Irian, as it is called by Indonesia. No sooner had Indonesia been granted independence by the Netherlands on December 27, 1949, than the newly created government demanded the transfer of West Irian to Indonesia. Bilateral negotiations were deadlocked. The matter was brought to the United Nations, where all attempts to find a peaceful settlement, to internationalize the problem, or to bring it before the International Court of Justice failed. It was obvious that Indonesia would not settle for less than immediate and full annexation of the area. It counted on the support of all Asian and African governments, as well as that of the Soviet Union, China and the United States of America. The Netherlands, with their pledge to grant the peoples of West New Guinea independence by 1970, found themselves completely isolated.

In this situation, Sukarno, the then ruler of Indonesia, opened what he himself called a confrontation in order to precipitate the decision; it turned out to be one of the most typical and most successful operations of its kind.

Strengthened by sizable deliveries of Soviet arms and some Chinese materiel, he assumed a threatening attitude against the Netherlands. Dutch property in Indonesia was confiscated in 1959; guerrilla forces were landed on the coasts of New Guinea or on the countless coastal islands. Many of the landing parties were rounded up by the Netherland's forces, but many more were able to infiltrate the country, and they succeeded in maintaining constant pressure on the colonial power. The certitude was created in the mind of the Dutch government and its allies that a full-fledged war was inevitable if the Netherlands did not yield to Indonesia's demands. A war for the last remains of the former empire of the Dutch Indies was out of the question, since this very empire had been given away under American and British pressure, and since West New Guinea was to have independence within ten years anyway. The United States, in turn, could not lightly tolerate an outbreak of war, since this would have placed them on the side of the opponents of the Netherlands. This might have had a disruptive effect on the North Atlantic Alliance. Moreover, Indonesia had been able to mobilize most countries to her cause to such an extent that Dutch troop reinforcements sent from Europe, had to reach the Far East by way of the West Indies and the Pacific Ocean, because of Indian, Japanese and African resistance.

When, on August 15, 1962, an agreement was signed in New York between the Netherlands and Indonesia, allowing the transfer of West Irian to Indonesia, a complicated procedure was devised by which the United States tried to veil the treason committed against the Papuas, the populations of West New Guinea. Their hope of gaining independence, similar to so many nations in Asia and Africa, was bitterly dashed. For a period of transition, the administration was to be laid in the hands of an organ of the United Nations, supported by the Indonesian forces which had already penetrated the country and some token forces from Malaysia. Six years later a plebiscite was to be held. Yet, no sooner had the U. N. token administration ended after little more than half a year, that Indonesia assumed full control of the country as the new colonial power.

The case is interesting, because it shows a perfect technique of confrontation, skillfully mixing military pressure with deterrent action and diplomatic maneuver. Indonesian diplomacy won the support of a large group of minor governments, the world powers and the United Nations bureaucracy in New York. When this support was not always unconditional, the opponent was at least made to believe that it was, and, therefore, to feel compelled to back down.

Indonesia continued its policy of confrontation. The Federation of Malaya was given independence in 1957 and was enlarged in 1963 by the inclusion of Singapore as well as Sarawak and Sabah on the Northern fringe of Borneo, to form Malaysia. Immediately, the victorious dictator of Indonesia turned his attention to this new goal of his appetite for conflict and perhaps conquest. Under the slogan *Ganjang Malaysia* (chew up Malaysia) he inaugurated a new confrontation, which he publicly advertised as such. He followed, in the process, the method applied so successfully with respect to West Irian.

Military pressure was applied by infiltrating Indonesian troops across the jungle border of Borneo into Sabah and Sarawak. Landings by sea were made nightly on the coast of the Straits of Malacca and on the thousand islands along the Malayan coast. The Soviet Union was mobilized diplomatically and gave its ready moral support. Moscow did not dare to antagonize the dictator in whom they had invested so much, lest he turn completely to the arch enemy, China. The usual campaign of propaganda among the developing countries began, this time against the "reactionary" government of Kuala Lumpur and the protector of Malaysia, Great Britain, accused of engaging in "neo-colonialist" activities. Despite the fact that Malaysia did not have the support of the average uncommitted, neutralist and otherwise anti-western governments of the developing world, and did not generally enjoy their sympathy, Indonesia did not succeed in creating a united front against its victim as in the case of West New Guinea. The United States was absent from the coalition, partly because of its wish not to antagonize London, partly because Malaysia had emerged successfully from a long struggle with communist subversion and infiltration. Therefore, Malaysia corresponded ideally to the American dream of independent Asian nations determined to resist communism, and it would have been paradoxical if Washington had taken sides against such a country.

If in Sukarno's second confrontation diplomatic support was much less effective than in the first one, military pressure proved to be a blunt weapon. Malaysia enjoyed the full support of Great Britain under a mutual defense agreement of 1957, and of Australia and New Zealand under earlier understandings. In contrast to the Dutch, the British had solid military bases in the area, Singapore and Hongkong. Most of the 18 battalions stationed in the area were experienced jungle troops. They were supported by an effective, diversified air force. Naval strength in the general area reached at one time as many as 80 ships, most of them small, yet very effective against the Indonesian infiltration tactics. The results of the Indonesian military pressure, accordingly, were not very impressive, and this in turn reflected on the diplomatic action. To be effective, confrontation seems to need two legs to stand on: An effective military posture and strong political support by third parties.

When the Indonesian infiltration by air and sea in August and September 1964 was brought before the Security Council of the United Nations, even two African states, Ivory Coast and Morocco, voted for a resolution critical of Indonesia. The Philippines, which have a claim on Sabah, did not look favorably on the possibility of the neighboring northern end of Borneo becoming part of Indonesia. In addition, governments like India's and Japan's, which had openly favored Indonesia in its confrontation with the Netherlands, showed growing uneasiness about the close links which developed between Indonesia and China and the support Sukarno received from Peking.

The strategic aims of Indonesia were not thought to be conquest and annexation of the whole of Malaysia, but rather the utter destruction of the Federal Union and the creation of a great many new states which could then be made satellites of Indonesia. This prospect was not welcome, of course, to the other governments in Asia. Therefore, Sukarno did not find the support necessary for a succesful operation.

The whole confrontation came to an end when in the night of September 30 to October 1st, 1965, the Communist party of Indonesia, abetted by Sukarno, tried to seize control by destroying the leaders of the armed forces, who had been for years the only power opposing the communists and balancing their ever growing influence in Indonesia. The *coup* failed. Sukarno was successively gradually divested of his functions by the victorious military leaders, who reversed the policy of the former regime and came to terms with Malaysia.

Sino-Soviet Confrontation

In the series of confrontations of our time those between Communist China and the Soviet Union occupy a dominant position. Invective, shows of force, including nuclear power, mutual pressure, competition for influence follow each other at such a pace, that it is difficult to distinguish one act from the next as isolated confrontations. Our object, therefore, is not to retrace the whole of the Sino-Soviet conflict, but rather to sketch how these incidents marking a mutual relationship dovetail into other confrontations we have described, how they are part of them, or how the adversaries use existing conflicts between third parties to build up positions to overtake the one real opponent.

When the guns of the People's Liberation Army on the Chinese mainland, in August, 1958, blazed away against the islands of Quemoi and Matsu, it could be construed as seen from the outside as an intensification of the confrontation between China and the government of Taipeh, and by proxy, between China and the United States. In reality, the thundering guns ushered in a new phase of the conflict between the two communist giants, the Union of Soviet Socialist Republics and the People's Republic of China. Within a few days, the Central Committee of the Chinese Communist Party proclaimed Mao Tse-tung as a high authority on Marxist thought. It proclaimed that China would take a short cut to communism by establishing the People's Communes. And it established itself as the true defender of the faith against the attempts by Khrushchev, who was seen with deep suspicion, to be seeking a tactical accommodation with the United States. The Chinese attitude of defiance towards the non-communist world, however, did not move Moscow to reverse its course and its new tactics; on the contrary, it confirmed it. China was punished for its attempt at questioning the absolute leadership of the Soviet Communist Party by the cancellation, in June 1959, of the agreement on technological help for the development of the Chinese atomic bomb. A year later the Russian experts were withdrawn, carrying with them the plans and blueprints for factories under construction, and throwing back the Chinese efforts at industrialization by years.

The conflict between the two rival communist powers tends to take the form of a triangular confrontation. While the "spirit of Camp David" was born and seemed to usher in a spectacular *rapprochement* between the Soviet Union and the United States of America, the Chinese accentuated their border conflict with India, and raised it in the winter of 1959-60 to the level of an armed clash. Thus China demonstrated its willingness to take risks and asserted its claim to leadership of the movement to establish socialism throughout the world, at least in the eyes of the developing nations. The impact on Soviet behavior of this pressure soon became apparent. The U-2 incident and its exploitation through the violent confrontation staged at the abortive meeting of heads of states in Paris in May 1960, was, at least in part, a concession to the onlooking Chinese rulers. The violence of the Soviet attempt to destroy the United Nations in the following September, in the wake of the Congo disaster of Soviet policy has to be explained, at least partly, by the pressure China exercised indirectly on Moscow.

When the conflict between the United States and the Soviet Union in 1961 and early 1962 assumed the form of a contest of nuclear explosions in the atmosphere, a kind of limited nuclear war, the Chinese, in view of this show of determination and violence on Moscow's side, seemed to retreat. A lull in the mutual recriminations set in; the two sides agreed that the open dispute should cease and that some kind of a world conference should be prepared to settle the dispute.

While the confrontation over Cuba still held the center of the stage, China re-opened its moves against India; these were designed to humiliate the rival Asian power, to ruin its influence in the developing world, and at the same time by proxy, its protector, the Soviet Union. Moscow reacted by deploring the Sino-Indian conflict and by withdrawing its support for a world communist conference. From then on, the situation between the two Communist parties deteriorated by leaps and bounds. A new lull intervened after October 14, 1964, when Khrushchev fell and was replaced by a triumvirate which seemed to be more restrained.

However, the disagreement over who should gain the decisive influence in Vietnam soon deeply involved the two governments. Demonstrations in front of their embassies were arranged. In August 1966 in the midst of the "Great Proletarian Cultural

Revolution," Mao Tse-tung was proclaimed the greatest Marxist-Leninist of our time. Beginning in early 1967 the conflict transcended the realm of the party quarrel, waged mainly in terms of competing ideologies, and became an open conflict between States. It assumed, to begin with, relatively mild forms of confrontation; demonstrations before their respective embassies were resumed. The Soviet Embassy in Peking was besieged from January 26 to February 13, 1967, and the Soviets retaliated with "spontaneous" demonstrations in front of the Chinese Embassy in Moscow. On June 17, 1967, the first Chinese thermonuclear bomb was exploded in Sinkiang, giving a somber background to the situation.

The conflict gradually assumed the aspects of a continuous confrontation, waged, however, with minor instruments which hardly correspond to the size of the powers involved and the interests for which they are fighting—ideological domination in the communist orbit, economic influence in the developing world. On March 2, 1969, a new stage was reached. Chinese and Soviet troops clashed on the Damansky Island in the Ussuri river which forms the border between Manchuria and the Soviet Costal Provinces on the Pacific Ocean. Exchanges of shots followed on the Amur river and in Sinkiang, with a major armed clash in the western region on August 13, 1969. Proof that these were more than border incidents, but rather moves in a fundamental confrontation, is the virulence of the mutual official protests, the explotation by the mass media, which bring the conflict into the open without restraint, and, which on the contrary, strive to present it in the most bloody, cruel way. The incidents were accompanied by demonstrations in front of embassies and significantly enough for the complex nature of confrontation, by negotiations started on June 22, 1969, in Chabarowsk and later in Peking.

On the ideological front, the Soviets gained a point by holding a world conference of their own, a *Concilium,* which opened on June 5, 1969. Originally designed as a forum for exposing Chinas "errors" and for undermining the position and prestige of the Chinese Communist party and Mao Tse-tung as one of the prophets of the movement, the effort fell short of this ultimate goal. The occupation of Czechoslovakia in the summer of 1968 had weakened Moscow's position to a point where it became impossible for its leaders to dominate the delegations. The introduction of armed forces and border clashes into the confrontation undermined the two contestant's position in the eyes of the other communist countries. This finds a significant expression in remarks in the Yugoslav *Review of International Affairs*:

> The border conflict between the big socialist states, and the possibility of a series of new conflicts combined with pressure, threats, etc., is rapidly destroying the myth of a special role of the socialist countries both in the struggle against imperialism and in the struggle for peace and active coexistence.[18]

Cyprus 1964 and 1967

It is not necessary to retrace the course and analyze all the minor confrontations of our time in which minor nations were engaged, since they do not add significant insights into the mechanism and the law of modern confrontation beyond and above the ones gained by examining a series of major and typical confrontations.

Mention must be made, however, of the most complex confrontation of recent years—that of Turkey and Greece over Cyprus. It is complex because of the historic background, the geographic location of the island and the ethnic composition of its population. Moreover, the case is complicated by the fact that three nations—Greece, Turkey and the United Kingdom—were primarily interested and involved, and by the fact that the two superpowers were deeply concerned over the outcome. Strong elements of intervention were combined throughout the struggle. In the complicated triangular—or rather pentagonal—diplomatic, political and strategic conflict all five governments took an active hand at varying stages. Yet only in the bilateral relationship of Turkey and Greece did the conflict become a confrontation.

---

[18] Bosko Siljegovic, "Communists and Conflicts," *Review of International Affairs* April 20, 1969 (Belgrade, 1969), transl. *Survival,* Vol. XI, No. 7, July 1969 (London, 1969), 218.

This occurred in December 1963 when the British troops stationed on the island were no longer able to prevent violence between Greek and Turkish Cypriotes. Turkey, on March 13, 1964, threatened to invade Cyprus in order to bring assistance to the hard pressed community of Turkish origin. The threat was withdrawn when the United Nations rushed the first elements of a peace force to the island. However, the military pressure by Turkey was gradually increased by gestures such as mobilization for invasion and overflights by military aircraft. This had an indirect effect: by June 1964 the Soviet Union finally reversed its opposition to the stationing of the United Nations Forces in Cyprus (UNFICYP), which had been sent there in March. The Soviet Union now supported their continued presence. This sudden change is explained by the fear of a NATO intervention; if a NATO presence on Cyprus could be avoided, the Soviet Union was willing even to tolerate an intervention by the United Nations.

However, the armed clashes between the two communities on the island continued, and the Turkish air force intervened by strafing and bombing Greek Cypriote positions. The super powers, fully aware of the implications of the deepening conflict and most anxious to avoid a confrontation between themselves, applied strong pressures on the Turks. On June 5, 1964, President Johnson sent a letter to Ankara, in which he threatened that Turkey might not receive NATO help in the event of a Soviet attack if her invasion of Cyprus were carried out.[19] On July 8, 1964, Khrushchev warned against a Turkish invasion and added that this would cause a dangerous chain reaction. President Johnson's letter, born out of the fear of worldwide complications, struck a blow to the relationship of trust and friendship between the United States and Turkey, from which it was never to recover; it was seized upon by Soviet diplomacy as the basis for opening a *rapprochement* with Turkey.

However, under such combined pressure, the Turkish threats subsided and there began a three year period of negotiations and attempts at mediation on different levels.

---

[19] T. W. Adam and Alvin J. Cottrell, *Cyprus Between East and West* (Baltimore, 1968), 37.

In November, 1967, when violence broke out again on
Cyprus, Turkey renewed her threats of invasion. She again announced a mobilization and her intention "to settle the problem
once and for all by partition of the island."[20] The threat accompanied and underlined four stern demands on the Greek
government. The Turkish position, in this new phase of the
confrontation, was much stronger than in 1964, because Ankara
had sought and obtained, after the fall of Khrushchev, a more
favorable attitude from Moscow. This time the United States
did not seem to be willing to interpose its Sixth Fleet, as in 1964,
against a Turkish operation. In 1964 such an interposition would
have been consonant with Soviet attitudes; in 1967 the Soviet
position had changed and by preventing invasion by force, the
United States would have pushed Turkey into the arms of the
Soviet Union.

War between Turkey and Greece now seemed possible; the
Turkish threat was credible, and this strengthened Turkey's
position decisively. Since war was to be prevented at any cost,
lest NATO suffer a humiliating blow, American and NATO
diplomacy began to exercise pressure on the Greek government.
In Athens, in the meantime, on April 21, 1967, power had been
usurped by a military group, which seemed, paradoxically, less
nationalistic and more realistic than the previous governments.
Under pressure, and probably also following its own preferences,
Athens yielded to Ankara's demands. The confrontation, conducted by Turkey with a skillful combination of threats of force
with diplomacy winning support or at least neutrality of the
superpowers, had been successful. It improved considerably the
situation of the Turkish community on Cyprus, yet did not bring
the basic problem any nearer to a solution.

In this context, Robert E. Osgood points to the paradox that
a major reason for the persistence of such conflicts is that the
super-powers try to prevent them from resulting in wars "which
are historically a primary means of settling such conflicts."[21]

---

20 *ibid.,* 71.
21 *ibid.,* vii.

Chapter V

The Concept Of Intervention

Terms and Definitions

For the purpose of this book, which is concerned with the study of contemporary use of force in an international environment in such a limited way as to keep the events under the control of the actors, the term "intervention" will be used in a well defined manner. As everyone knows, the word may carry ambiguous and imprecise meanings such as to describe any action affecting the interests of others. Even in the literature of political science and law we find a rather free-wheeling usage.

We view intervention here as a specific kind of strategic action. It is strategic in the wide sense of the combination of policy with power. And it is distinguished from other international situations or actions, in which will stands against will, force against force (as for instance confrontation), by five special features. These features are:

First. The act is designed, at least in the eyes of the intervening power, to uphold some established rule of politics, morality or law.

Second. The power relationship between the intervenor and the intervened is such that the first is distinctly superior to the second.

Third. The behavior of the intervenor is such as to differ sharply from the attitudes adopted up to the intervention.

Fourth. The act is limited in scope and in time; it "intervenes" between other phases of the relationship.

83

Fifth. The act is addressed to the political structure of the nation or society which is the object of the intervention, and it is not relevant whether it has been invited or not.

Hence, we are dealing with situations or actions in which one superior nation or an international organization or a multinational combination of states transcends the framework of the existing relations and attempts to impose its will on a weaker nation in defense of some concept of a political, moral or legal order, and with a limited duration in mind.

This definition also settles the problem of intervention by request of the intervened. It is often argued that intervention may take place with the consent or by invitation of the state which is the target of the action. In practice, the argument that an intervention has been requested is frequently used as a justification. In these cases, the element of opposing wills would be lacking, and, therefore, there is no question of intervention, but rather of assistance, help, of co-operation, of treaty relationship such as an alliance of mutual assistance or similar patterns of international relations. As an example we may cite the Security Treaty between Japan and the United States of September 8, 1951.

The term "intervention" is, of course, often used in a much wider yet less precise way. Some analysts are inclined to term any foreign policy behavior as interventionary when a power tries to change the behavior of another power. This concept is much too broad, so broad as to include almost any type of international conflict. Further, when a nation takes sides in an already existing conflict, the act is often described as "intervention," analagous to its use in legal terminology.

The right of the International Committee of the Red Cross to make representations under the Geneva Conventions of 1949 for the protection of victims of armed conflicts is, in legal literature, called "intervention." Its action in fulfillment of a humanitarian task which is not supported by any political power is, of course, not intervention in the strict sense of the term.[1]

---

[1] Paul Guggenheim, *Lehrbuch des Völkerrechts* (Basel, 1951), 807.

Some authors have used the term simply as an equivalent to a military *coup d'etat*.

Among the many useful attemps made to narrow the definition of intervention, in order to allow a meaningful discussion, one of them seems to carry special weight. The author describes as interventionary the behavior of an international actor towards another whenever "the form of the behavior constitutes a sharp break with the then-existing forms *and* whenever it is directed at changing or preserving the structure of political authority in the target society."[2]

This description of intervention is very much in agreement with the formulation suggested above, with the only difference that it does not mention the power relationship, in which the intervenor is relatively superior to the intervened. Nevertheless, this specific power relationship is essential to the concept of intervention.

Another author emphasizes that intervention should always refer to organized and systematic activities, and always to activities across recognized boundaries. He would not consider clashes over disputed territory as cases of intervention.[3]

For our part, we are dealing exclusively with relationships between states and not between individuals, political parties, private groups or organizations, or between such elements and states. This should be perfectly clear. Interventions may, of course, be undertaken by bodies which are not visibly part of a governmental authority or of its armed forces. This will be the case in most instances of infiltration and subversion. Yet it is essential to the conceptual pattern of intervention that a link exist between such organizations and a higher authority. Therefore, for instance, the subversive and terroristic activities in the Italian provinces forming the region of Alto Adige, or South Tyrol, will not be considered and described as interventions. This in spite of the fact that at certain times local Austrian and German authorities have abetted such activities.

---

[2] James N. Rosenau, "The Concept of Intervention," *Journal of International Affairs,* Vol. XXII, No. 2 (New York: School of International Affairs Columbia University, 1968), 165.

[3] Oran R. Young, "Intervention and International Systems," *Journal of International Affairs,* Vol. XXII, No. 2, 178.

Similarly political murder, even when organized and ordered by high authority, such as the assassination of the Ukrainian
nationalist leaders, Rebet and Bandera in 1957 and 1959 in
Munich by the Soviet agent Bodgan Stanshinskij, will not be
listed under intervention. All activities such as espionage and
related methods are equally excluded from the concept of intervention.

We shall now deal one by one with the features listed above,
which distinguish intervention from other activities of an antagonistic nature in international relationship.

Lofty goals

Nations have always tried to find for their actions, even for
those dictated by self interest or still less commendable motivations, some high sounding title or reason to justify them in the
eyes of the world, the victim, or of their own conscience. This
belongs to the normal and age-old field of propaganda, political
psychology and psychological warfare. In such a case nobody
is expected to believe all of what is being said.

In the case of intervention the situation is different. Here
the actors seem to agree that some universally accepted principle,
an ideology, a legal order, a commandment of morality or religion, or an ideal world order has to be established or upheld.
So strong is this impulse that in many cases even the victim seems
to agree on the validity of the general claims of the intervening
power or powers, however deep the opposition to the methods
applied or the right of the intervenor to act as the representative
of the alleged principles may be.

This concept found its almost classic expression in the
treaties, conferences and declarations based on the treaty of
November 20, 1815, in which Russia, Austria, Prussia and Great
Britain set up what is commonly called the Holy Alliance as a
basis for intervention against revolutionary movements. Its leading doctrine was expressed in Metternich's circular dispatch of
May 12, 1821, when he said:

> Useful or necessary changes in the governments of states must emanate
> only from the free will and the thoughtful and enlightened initiative
> of those whom God has made responsible for power. [The powers]

will consider void, and contrary to the principles of the *public law* of Europe, all pretended reforms brought about by revolution, or by force,"[4]

Even after the Holy Alliance, which had never been a real alliance or an effective instrument but rather a political theory, had definitely collapsed in the revolutionary storms of 1848, the conceptual framework of intervention, which had found expression in it, survived. The almost mystical treaty which had prepared it had been based on the Christian faith. Christianity and Christian ethics continued to be at the basis of the philosophy of intervention. It was universally believed that the European great powers represented enlightened civilization, humanitarian ideals and a firm domestic order, which was the most favorable condition for international order. These lofty ideals and convictions were brought into sharp contrast to the backwardness, ignorance, impotence, instability and generally immoral qualities of smaller nations and especially those which were not white, European or North American. While the United States moved to become a great power, it also eagerly espoused such views and principles.

The declining Ottoman Empire and the atrocities committed during the ensuing period of anarchy against minorities gave, throughout the nineteenth century, ample occasion for the application of interventionary doctrines. The plight of Christians was the usual pretext for armed interventions, such as from 1827 to 1830 in Greece, and from 1876 to 1878 in Bulgaria, Serbia, Rumania and Montenegro. The outcome was most often territorial annexation or the creation of independent states with regimes favorable to the intervenors. How the fate of the supposedly rescued minorities was affected, usually remained a matter of minor concern. When in 1860 six thousand Maronite Christians were murdered in Syria by the Druses, Austria, France, Great Britain, Russia and Turkey concluded in Paris the convention of September 5, 1860, which authorized France to intervene by force. French troops occupied Syria from August, 1860 to June, 1861 and laid the basis for the autonomy of Lebanon and for dominant French influence in the area for almost a century. The

---

[4] Martens, *Nouveau Recueil*, Vol. V, 644.

term "humanitarian intervention" was, in the process, introduced into political terminology.[5]

President Theodore Roosevelt gave forceful expression to
the conviction that a great power had the right and the duty
to intervene, when he said in his forth Annual Message to the
Congress, on December 6, 1904:

> Brutal wrongdoing, or an impotence which results in a general
> loosening of the ties of civilized society, may in America, as elsewhere,
> ultimately require intervention by some civilized nation, and in the
> Western Hemisphere the adherence of the United States to the
> Monroe Doctrine may force the United States, however reluctantly,
> in flagrant cases of such wrongdoing or impotence, to the exercise
> of its international police power.[6]

Up to 1914 the possession of the Christian faith decisively
strengthened the title which a power could invoke when she
acted as the guardian of right and law. When, after 1918, Japan
joined the ranks of the surviving great powers, Christianity became a less obvious prerequisite of the great power status which
bestows the right to intervene. A Christian power, Germany was,
at the same time, eliminated from the ranks of the "happy few,"
since it was held responsible for the war and for such international wrongdoing considered incompatible with the special
qualities of a responsible great power.

The right to act as the international policeman was not con-
fined to the great powers. A corresponding role could be assumed
by any other nation as long as it was considered civilized.
However, there was a kind of "pecking order" established among
the nations. It finds classical expression in the remarks of an
American author, who represents the traditional imperialistic
views, almost naïvely, in their purest form, Ellery C. Stowell.
He wrote that:

> . . .any state may . . . proceed against the delinquent state to obtain
> redress, provided always that a reasonable opportunity is afforded
> to the paramount state to undertake itself the burden of exacting

[5] Andres Davila, *Humanitarian Intervention in Public International Law*
(Geneva: Institut Universitaire de Hautes Etudes Internationales Dipl. No. 96,
1967).

[6] *The State of the Union Messages of the Presidents 1790-1966* (New York,
1966), 2134.

on the part of its ward a compliance with its international obligations.[7]

The end of World War I brought a deep change in the ideological background for intervention. The social order within the nations had been profoundly affected by the sufferings of the war, and, even more, by the fact that the ruling or otherwise influential groups had not been able to prevent the catastrophe from happening. The authority of the great powers, which had been unchallenged throughout the epoch of empire building and empire administrating, had been undermined by the very powers themselves. By engaging in a self-destructive war they had forfeited their right to police the world. The British Navy, for almost a century the policeman of the world, was replaced by the legalistic framework of collective security and peace through law, as administrated by the League of Nations and the Permanent Court of International Justice. The great powers which had precariously survived the great tragedy continued, in a rather uncertain way, to set the standards of international behavior and to rule the world, after a fashion, through the weak instrument of the League. The United States, aloof from the League and withdrawn from global responsibility, firmly established its role of policing power for the whole of the Western Hemisphere and wide expanses of the Pacific Ocean. It was not surprising though, that the system was finally destroyed by a power which had only recently and very reluctantly been admitted to the ruling group, Japan, and by a former member which had been humiliated and excluded, Germany.

Intervention, in the process, lost the splendor and majesty which it had enjoyed in the period when the imperial powers, however divided and jealous for any other purpose, had united to raise the one and single voice of the civilized world. They could no longer seek and find redress by a solemn salute to their flag or elaborate excuses and expiatory gestures. It was a far cry from the time when in December, 1900, during their intervention in China to suppress the Boxer uprising, eleven nations signed a joint note to the Emperor of China, enjoining

---

[7] Ellery C. Stowell, *Intervention in International Law* (Washington, D.C., 1921), 306.

him to send a mission to Berlin to express apologies for the murder in Peking of the German minister, Baron von Ketteler, and to erect a monument on the place of the murder, with an inscription in German, Chinese and Latin, expressing the deep regret of the Emperor of China.[8] Intervention became, in the time between the two World Wars, a rather narrow and egoistic means to secure certain advantages for a nation or for its nationals, exercised in a rather cynical way.

After World War II the political, moral and legal background of intervention again changed. The motivation and justification by lofty concepts like civilization, Christianity, public international law had, until then, been a solid body of ideas, to which everyone seemed to adhere. It split now into two distinct concepts, deeply opposed to each other.

Intervention, from then on, has evolved in two entirely distinct patterns, represents two different political systems, and obeys two entirely different sets of inspiration. What the two systems have in common is the fact that both profess to seek a lofty goal and both lay claim to universal validity.

The United States, and to a lesser degree Great Britain and France, remained to carry the old banner of law and order in international relations, most of the time by the intermediary of the instruments of the United Nations, into the lands of the infidels. The lofty goal was summarized in the words freedom, democracy, self-determination. Intervention, from 1945, as practiced mainly by the United States but also in a more limited way by Great Britain and France, was aimed at supporting or establishing governments which would adhere to the ideals of democracy, national independence, free enterprise, as opposed to communist-oriented governments.

A new power had emerged after World War II with entirely different concepts and ideals. The Soviet Union came out of the war with greatly increased political and military might and with a considerably increased appeal of its ideology. The banner under which she was to intervene in foreign countries and to participate in the contest for international influence was that of scientific

---

[8] ibid., 30.

Marxism-Leninism. She was pledged to the promise of a future better world order under the dictatorship of the laboring classes.

The Soviet Union has based the right to intervene, repeatedly used, on the sacred duty to prevent counter-revolution. The lofty goal is to sustain the struggle between two opposing social systems—capitalism and socialism. As the pronouncement thought to be most authoritative and currently referred-to as the Brezhniew Doctrine[9] has it, the sovereignty of each socialist country cannot be opposed to the interests of the socialist world and the interests of the world revolutionary movement. Socialist countries owe their national independence to the might of the socialist community and, above all, to the Soviet Union as its central force, including its armed forces. The Soviet Union, therefore, would fail to discharge its obligation towards the working classes and the socialist community if it did not intervene wherever "counter-revolution" seemed to threaten the achievements of revolution.

Inequality of power

Whatever may be the banner under which nations strive to impose their views on other nations and to try to bring about the ideal world order which they profess, the instrument of intervention will never be employed against an equal or a stronger nation. If, throughout the centuries, intervention has seemed less objectionable than stark aggression or attack and has been supported by public international law, which began to distinguish between legitimate and illegitimate intervention, it was partly due to the ideological justification described in the preceding section. Even more powerful though than ideology for making intervention respectable was the consensus that only great powers or powerful international organizations are authorized to wield this instrument of policy, and only vis-a-vis their inferiors. This consensus can be explained by the pattern of authority which underlies the whole institution. Authority evidently only exists when a power relationship places the one actor above the other. The bigger the difference between the size and power of the

---

[9] Sergei Kovalyov, "Sovereignty and International Duties," *Pravda*, September 26, 1968, transl. *Survival*, Vol. X, No. 11, November, 1968 (London, 1968), 375.

intervening nation and the power of its opponent, the more intervention has seemed morally and legally justified as an act in defense of international order and legality. It signalled that a great power had "taken the law in its own hands." This was called by Theodore Roosevelt the "proper international relations between the strong and the weak."[10]

As intervening powers we can distinguish individual nations and collectivities, such as *ad hoc* constituted groups of sovereign states or international organizations. From the very beginning of intervention in modern times—remember the Holy Alliance—collective acts were the preferred form. One of the reasons was that inequality of power and the overwhelming strength of the intervenor or intervenors was considered an essential requirement. Other reasons for the tendency towards collective intervention were the legal and moral aspects. Such aggressive actions seemed less objectionable when conducted in the name of a collectivity.

It never occurred to anyone that a great power might intervene in the affairs of another great power and consequently much less that any smaller nation might intervene against a great power. The only apparent exception was the intervention of the Allied powers in Russia from 1917 to 1921. As we later will see the situation at the time was such that the normal standards of size did not apply. When great powers did not agree and tried to obtain concessions or change between one another, it simply meant conflict, confrontation, war.

This conviction was universally shared by large and small nations. For the great powers it represented the system of imperialistic rule, to which they themselves adhered and which served their interests so well. For the smaller nations it represented at least some kind of international order, which in most cases, when they were not directly affected by an interventionary move, gave them protection. Sheltered by this system, they could comfortably do business. Nations like the Netherlands, Belgium, Portugal, Denmark, which under the system were able to maintain large colonial empires, or other nations like Sweden, Norway,

---

[10] A. B. Hart and H. R. Ferleger, *Theodore Roosevelt Cyclopedia* (New York, 1941), 551.

Switzerland, which extended and exploited their world wide business relations, give ample proof of the advantages this international order had for small European nations, in spite of its inherent injustice. The system was at a time when it had already become obsolete, poignantly characterized in a judgment of the International Court of Justice rendered in 1949 in the Corfu Channel Case. The Court stated that the case had been presented by the United Kingdom as a new and special application of the theory of intervention, and then went on to say:

> The Court can only regard the alleged right of intervention as the manifestation of a policy of force, such as has, in the past, given rise to most serious abuses and such as cannot, whatever be the defects in international organization, find a place in international law. Intervention is perhaps still less admissible in the particular form it would have taken here; for, from the nature of things, it would be reserved for the most powerful States, . . .[11]

This judgment is equivalent to the assertion that, if the argument that superior power entitles to international executive authority is held invalid and inadmissible, the whole institution of intervention collapses.

Dramatic change, Limitation in Scope and Time

Intervention does not exist when a relationship between nations, one small and the other more powerful, is equivalent to a permanent relationship of influence exercised on the smaller nation. The relationship between the Soviet Union and the European nations members of the Warsaw Pact are a telling example. Through the instruments of the Communist parties, which are closely linked at the top, through close links existing between the planned state economies, and through the common military command, the behavior of the countries, which are frequently called the "satellites," is deeply and permanently affected by the views prevailing in the Soviet Union. This influence is not considered to be interventionary.

It is only when a new element dramatically comes to alter the previous behavior that the picture changes. On June 17, 1953, workers demonstrations at the Stalin Allee in East Berlin

---

[11] "The Corfu Channel Case: Merits, Judgment of April 9, 1949," *International Court of Justice Reports 1949*, 35.

against the 10 percent increase of work norms expanded and became manifestations against the regime of the Deutsche Demokratische Republik, spreading over wide areas. When the German police proved powerless or unreliable, the Soviet Army put down the movement by force. At this very moment, the relationship had become interventionary. Intervention ceased when calm was restored and the leaders of the revolutionary movement had been arrested and executed.

In October 1956 when the agitation of young Hungarian workers and students, modelled after a similar movement in Poland, turned into a national uprising against the communist regime led by E. Gero, and later by the former head of government Imre Nagy, the Soviet Army entered Budapest and occupied the capital. Fighting went on in many areas until November 13. The leaders of the movement, including Nagy, were arrested and later executed. Soviet influence and leadership had turned into intervention.

In Czechoslovakia, the presence of Soviet troops under the terms of the Warsaw Pact was part of the existing close relationship of a small communist country within the orbit of the communist world power and its dependence on the Soviet Union. Even military staff maneuvers of Warsaw Pact armies, which took place in early summer of 1968, in spite of being clearly intended as a signal or a threat to the authorities in Prague, were not considered as an intervention, since they corresponded in their outward forms very much to the *courant normal* of the relationship. It needed the sudden penetration of Soviet forces in Czechoslovakia, the seizing of key points in Prague and other cities in the early hours of August 21, 1968, to make the Soviet behavior interventionary. These characteristics subsided despite the continued presence of Soviet forces on Czech territory, when the party and government authorities had been reshaped according to the demands of Moscow and the liberalization course had been reversed.

Under the doctrines developed in the United States in the second half of the 19th century and early 20th century, the nations of Central and South America were actually regarded as being under the permanent protection and guard of the United

States. The Latin Americans sharply criticized and resisted this doctrine, but it took almost a century for their views to prevail. The North American influence was actually so strong in some of the Central American Republics, that the US Embassy or Legation was considered the tutor of the government. These republics were, in North American eyes, free and sovereign, but, so to say, "on probation." President Theodore Roosevelt expressed this clearly in his Second Annual Message of December 2, 1902, when he said:

> It behooves each one to maintain order within its own borders and to discharge its just obligations to foreigners. When this is done, they can rest assured that, be they strong or weak, they have nothing to dread from outside interference.[12]

This relationship is not regarded as interventionary, except in political rhetorics. The United States landed troops in Columbia, on the Isthmus of Panama often in 1856, 1860, 1873, 1885, 1901, 1902. Yet even these military steps were hardly considered as interventionary; they were part of the assistance normally given to the Columbian government in policing that vulnerable area. When Nicaragua was occupied by US Marines from 1912 to August 1925, one hardly thought of intervention, or rather, the fact that intervention had taken place, was conveniently forgotten.

However, when a rebellion in the city of Panama, on November 3, 1903, broke out and independence of the area from Columbia was declared, United States forces, landed from a warship, prevented the Columbian army from putting down the independence movement. Three days later Washington hastily recognized the new Republic of Panama. This was clearly and correctly considered an intervention, since the United States first by subversion and then by force of arms had broken up the political integrity of Columbia for its own advantage.

In the course of this special relationship, which existed for more than a century between the Central American Republics and their great neighbor in the north, it was customary to speak of intervention only when the normal course of events was dramatically altered. It was generally the "Landing of the Ma-

---

[12] *The State of the Union Messages,* 2062.

rines" which caused that alteration and signalled that intervention was taking place.

This feature of intervention is intimately linked with the requirement that it be limited in scope and in time. The beginning can clearly be distinguished, since it requires breaking the normal forms of intercourse between the two nations concerned. The end often comes only gradually. We discover that intervention has come to an end when the intervening forces are withdrawn, or when their presence has become a permanent feature, or when the aim of the intervention is achieved, or when the operation has been unsuccessful and is discontinued.

The victim of intervention may, when the operation is accomplished, recover its independence and full sovereignty, or it may remain under the lasting influence of the intervening power. Then, however, the situation changes into one of occupation, one of colonial or imperialistic rule.

Similarly, the sudden cancellation by the United States and Britain of the promises of assistance to Egypt in building the Aswan High dam, on July 20, 1956, was probably thought to deal a deadly blow to Colonel Gamal Abdel Nasser's prestige, to cause his fall and to encourage his replacement by a government easier to deal with. It certainly can be considered as an intervention, however limited and unsuccessful it may have been.

Another form of dramatic change may also be the transition from a bilateral relationship between two antagonists to a relationship between a collectivity and the target society. The sudden introduction of collective action, as in the case of China at the beginning of the 20 century, is an instance of the convention-breaking behavior required by the definition of intervention.

It is typical of intervention that its scope is limited. The payment of a debt, the security of a minority, the punishment of a wrongdoer, the liberation of a prisoner, the overthrow of a government or the defeat of a revolutionary movement—all of these are typical limited objects of intervention. When an operation goes beyond such limited and well-defined objects one would not speak of intervention but rather of an aggression, a war of conquest.

Dramatic change as a prerequisite to the existence of intervention most frequently comes about as the deployment and application of military force. It is the most visible, most dramatic form of intervention. But it is not the only form. Abruptly discontinuing a foreign aid program may well be considered as a kind of intervention; its purpose—to alter the power structure of the target society—may well be achieved by this method.

In 1936 the Spanish government in a note addressed to the French government described the interruption of arms shipments to Madrid in a critical phase of the civil war as a "very effective intervention in the domestic affairs of Spain."

When the Soviet Union, on June 20, 1959, cancelled the agreement with China to help her in building the atomic bomb and the corresponding delivery systems and a year later withdrew all Soviet industrial experts, the thrust certainly was aimed not only at a technological project or at industrialization, but at the very heart of Chinese power. The Soviet Union hoped to bring about the downfall of a government whose stability was already shaken by the failure of the great leap forward.

Thrust at the Political Structures

Most interventions naturally aim at modifying the political structure, by changing the seat of power in the target nation, since such dramatic steps are generally not taken by a government if it does not want to achieve a significant change. These operations are readily recognizable as such when they use the instruments of military threat or force or open diplomatic, political or economic pressure.

They may be much more difficult to discover when they are disguised. One of the most frequently observed methods of disguise is the argument that the intervention has been made on request.

The argument that an intervention has been requested or invited and therefore is no intervention at all will aways prove irrelevant and can safely be ignored. Unless a permanent relationship of cooperation exists between the parties concerned which eliminates the element of opposing sovereignties and the clash of will and, therefore, excludes the concept of intervention, the argument of invitation has to be ignored. In practice it will never safely be ascertained whether the request or the invitation was actually issued, and if it was, whether or not it came from a competent authority. Intervention may equally appear in disguise when it assumes the forms of cultural or political propaganda, or the forms of economic and technological cooperation. Then it is considerably more difficult to decide whether or not we are in the presence of intervention.

The essential factor for the assessment of such actions will always be that they are aimed, openly or in disguise, at the authority structures of the target nation. We would not think and speak of intervention in the many cases where a government tries to shape things, across an international border, by addressing itself directly to the problem. To favor investment in order to gain control of the economy or parts of the economy of another country, even if operated by government authority, is certainly not interventionary in the correct meaning of the word. Deployment of propaganda means in order to win the favor of the public, or to encourage development of certain elements of the infrastructure which may be highly favorable to the foreign governments, certainly is not intervention. A railroad of greatest strategic value may be built in a foreign country, for example, on the pattern of the French and German-sponsored Anatolian Railways and the Bagdad Railway (1903-1918), or the Chinese-built railway in East Africa from Dar es Salaam to Lusaka in Zambia (1967). It is not intervention, when achieved through instruments not aimed at the power structure of the receiving country.

On the other hand we speak of intervention when the operation is being conducted through the government of the target country and when this government has been changed in its composition or influenced in its decisions in order to achieve the final aim. A typical example of such interventionary policy is the building of the Panama Canal; in 1903 the United States favored the elimination of Colombian sovereignty over the Isthmus and helped to set up an independent government with which the treaty for the building and exploitation of the canal could be conveniently negotiated. Another example, already mentioned, is the cancellation of the help to Egypt for the building of the Aswan High dam by the western powers; this act was aimed at altering the power structures of the republic.

Having thus characterized intervention as an operation, limited in scope and time, conducted by a stronger nation against a weaker one, opened by a sharp break in behavior and addressed to the power structure in the target society, and always conducted in the name of some higher principle, for contrast's sake it remains to point to some historical events which may not be termed interventions.

The acts of colonial conquest in the eighteenth, nineteenth and twentieth centuries do not fall under the definition of intervention, since they were aimed at establishing a permanent relationship. The building of the Russian colonial empire in Central Asia, Siberia and the Far East was a series of acts of imperialistic conquest. The many military operations of the French and the British in India may have appeared at the time to have features of interventionary operations, yet they were linked by the fact that they led finally towards permanent domination and annexation. The opening of Japan to world trade through demonstrations of force by Russian and American warships outwardly looks like a borderline case of intervention, but the scope was wide and unlimited in time, and the demonstrations did no more than accelerate an historic development which was already in the making and which provided Japan with a new power structure. Therefore, it is not really a case of intervention. The occupation of Mexico by French armies from 1861 to 1867 was an attempt at territorial conquest which in its proportions widely transcends the domain of intervention. When the United States took sides against Spain during the Cuban rebellion which had started in 1895, and where she declared war on Spain on April 25, 1898, it was really a war of conquest which had been encouraged by the deep crisis shaking at that time the remains of the Spanish colonial empire. The war led to the conquest of Cuba, Puerto Rico and the Philippines. The French penetration in Morocco, which began in earnest in 1907, after the conference of Algeciras had given France the green light, was styled an intervention for the pacification of the country. It started with the bombardment of Casablanca and the landing of a French division, but it was not really an intervention, since the operations were initiated for the permanent conquest of the country. Similarly the Japanese operations against China, started in 1931, 1932 and 1937 in the disguise of interventions, immediately transcended, by leaps and bounds, such a limited undertaking; it developed into a great war of conquest which was to last until 1945. The same is true for the Italian conquest of Ethiopia, initiated on October 3, 1935.

The massive assistance given to the government of China by the United States in the form of munitions, economic help and advice during World War II was not intervention, since the operation was part of warfare by an alliance against Japan. The attempt at mediation between Nationalists and Communists in China, which was entrusted to General Marshall in the years 1945 to 1946, was intimately linked with the preceding war effort; the operation in China will therefore not be numbered among interventions.

Among the numerous pretexts for conquest and the countless disguises under which wars were begun, the claim that an intervention was necessary is almost a classical one. However, having in mind the definition of intervention, it is easy to distinguish territorial conquest from this much more limited form of conflict.

Chapter VI

Interventions Before World War II

Humanitarian and Not So Humanitarian

To understand fully the politics underlying intervention in our time and the evolution of international public law related to the institution, it is necessary to look back at a few of the more striking instances of an interventionary character in modern history.

In the nineteenth century and the early twentieth century, governments of large or smaller nations repeatedly took forcible action to protect their interests, the interests of their nationals or the interests of nationals of the target country thought to be unjustly or inhumanly treated; or they also took action to revenge an "affront and indignity"[1] against a power or one of its nationals, or to suppress slave trade or piracy. So frequently, indeed, did they act that no one seems ever to have attempted counting and listing these actions. Many of these unilateral acts were termed humanitarian interventions and as such considered permissible in spite of the fact that they often led to abuses.

One of the more spectacular instances, known for its brutality and the applause it earned as a "just" act, was the bombardment and subsequent burning of San Juan, or Greytown, in Nicaragua, on July 13, 1854, by the Commander of the U.S. warship *Cyane,* in retaliation for damages inflicted on American citizens and for "indignities offered to the U.S. in the person of her accredited minister."[2] In 1901 Germany, Italy and Great Britain blockaded the ports of Venezuela with their naval forces

[1] Resolution of the Congress of the US April 22, 1914, *38 US Statutes at Large,* 770.

[2] "Perrin v. United States," *4 Court of Claims Reports,* 543.

101

in order to collect a public debt. For similar reasons, the Netherlands destroyed Venezuela's fleet in 1908.

Cuba offers particular interest, since the United States demanded and, based on the Platt Amendment of March 2, 1901, obtained the insertion in the Cuban constitution of a provision expressly authorizing intervention in the domestic affairs of the Republic,[3] and a corresponding treaty. The United States actually made use of this right obtained by pressure; it intervened in the domestic troubles of the new Republic, and occupied Cuba from 1903 to 1906.

The many interventions in the affairs of Colombia, which culminated in 1903 in the establishment of the Republic of Panama and the consequent building of the transcontinental canal, have been mentioned earlier. Mexico, Nicaragua, Haiti, the Dominican Republic, all were at times fully or partially occupied by forces of the United States.

China offers a long and unhappy history of interventions by Russia, Great Britain, France, the United States and Germany.[4] The highlights are the treaty of Tientsin of 1858, forced upon China by Lord Elgin; the British and French occupation of Peking, in 1860, with the burning down of the Summer Palace; and the "Boxer" uprising in 1900-01, during which the Embassy quarter established in 1860 was attacked by the revolutionary forces and which was answered by a multinational intervention or punishing expedition.

Japan had forced upon China in 1915 and 1922 treaties which entitled her to administer a zone along the South Manchurian railway. An incident of September 18, 1931, gave the pretext for the Japanese occupation of the whole of Manchuria, which was termed a "provisional intervention." The operation was followed, on January 19, 1932, by a Japanese-arranged incident in Shanghai which led to the landing of troops, severe fighting and the occupation of a large area of China. Based on the treaty ending the Boxer intervention, the Japanese maintained armed forces in the vicinity of Peking. On July 7, 1937,

---

[3] David F. Haley, *The United States in Cuba* 1898-1902 (Madison, Wisconsin, 1963), 150.

[4] Pierre Renouvin, *La Question d'Extrême-Orient 1840-1940* (Paris, 1946).

during maneuvers of these forces, the Japanese provoked an incident at the Marco Polo bridge, which by demands impossible to meet they transformed into confrontation and the confrontation into war.

A typical case of humanitarian intervention was the initiative taken by the United States and Great Britain in 1911 against Peru to stop atrocities against the Indians committed in Putamayo on the Upper Amazon River. The U.S. and Britain demanded an investigation and the trial of the persons responsible. The pressure applied was not military power but a conference forced upon the President of Peru and the threat to publicize the reports on Putamayo.[5]

Soviet Russia

From November 1917 to 1920 France, Great Britain, the United States of America, Japan, Polish and Czechoslovak military forces and some of the other Allies—twelve participants altogether—intervened in Russia. When the Tsar abdicated on March 16, 1917, the Allies first hoped for an improvement of the Russian war effort against Germany, Austria and Turkey. However, the Russian front crumbled, and after the Bolsheviks had seized power on November 6 and 8, the armistice of Brest Litowsk of December 15, 1917 practically ended Russian participation in the war. It was natural that the Allies, hard-pressed on the Western front and in Italy, would try to re-establish an Eastern front. Japanese and Czechoslovak forces were expected to move in from Siberia and British, French and American troops from the Arctic ports and from the Middle East. In May 1918 the United States landed troops in Murmansk and Archangelsk. The northern operation was first described as a design to protect the Arctic ports against German and Finnish invasion, and great care was taken to remain on friendly terms with Lenin's government, always in the hope that the Bolsheviks, now "Communists," could be won to participate again on the side of the "democratic" powers against German imperialism.

---

[5] Ellery C. Stowell, *Intervention in International Law* (Washington, D.C., 1921), 179.

In July, the British invaded Turkestan, and in December 1918 they landed forces in Odessa and Sebastopol.

However, the new Russian government was uncooperative and concluded peace, on March 3, 1918, in Brest Litowsk, with Germany. Gradually, the operations first designed to establish a second front became an intervention on the side of the many and conflicting counter-revolutionary forces against the Bolshevik government, in the hope that it would be overthrown and that Russia could be brought back into the war. After the collapse of Germany on November 11, 1918, the operations, conducted with weak and inadequate forces in the wide expanses of Russia, became entirely policy-oriented and therefore fully acquired the character of an intervention. It was broken off, beginning in 1919, when it appeared that nothing short of all-out war against Russia would assure the victory of the counter revolutionaries in the civil war. The Japanese were the last to evacuate their forces; they left Vladivostok as late as October 1922.[6]

Some authors believe that the strategic move, designed as a war effort against Germany and Austria and then transformed into intervention, far from weakening the communist government, greatly contributed toward its strengthening and final success. The struggle had given it the argument that it was waging a patriotic war and had compelled it to build a strong army and an efficient police force.[7]

Intervention v. Non-Intervention—The Spanish Civil War

When on July 17, 1936, a group of Spanish military commanders took up arms, first in Spanish Morocco and later on the peninsula, to overthrow the government in Madrid, one of the most sanguinary civil wars of modern history started, and, along with it, a complex series of interventions. Both Italy and Germany realized that an occasion presented itself to overthrow a government of leftist orientation. They also hoped to establish a government on the fascist and national-socialist pattern, national-

---

[6] Richard H. Ullman, *Intervention and the War, Anglo-Soviet Relations 1917-1921* (Princeton, New Jersey, 1961).

[7] Herbert S. Dinerstein, *Intervention Against Communism* (Baltimore: Washington Center of Foreign Policy Research, 1967), 6.

istic, militaristic and aggressive, and perhaps a useful ally in future conflicts. They decided to intervene.

Italian intervention started, upon a request presented in Rome on July 19, by providing air transport for General Francisco Franco, who, at the head of troops from Spanish Morocco, landed in Andalusia. When the military *coup* did not succeed within a few days, as had been expected, the intervenor was gradually drawn into the ensuing civil war. Italy dispatched to Spain as many as four divisions, claimed to be divisions of volunteers, together with the corresponding supporting forces to Spain. They conducted independent operations, such as the occupation of the northern provinces, and a special attack on Madrid. Germany provided, starting in August, under the thin disguise of a "volunteer" organization, called *Legion Condor,* bomber and fighter forces, anti-aircraft artillery, a communications system and naval support to the party headed by General Franco.

The French government sent, or sold, against payment in gold, approximately one hundred airplanes to the Madrid government. Most of them were operated by a voluntary organization set up in France by André Malraux. The International Brigades, organized in France, proved to be a decisive element. They were composed of true volunteers, Italian and German emigrees, idealistic anti-fascists of many nations, writers like George Orwell, unemployed, adventurers, refugees from dictatorially-governed Eastern European countries. No Russians were allowed to join as volunteers, yet the whole force was firmly under communist authority and command. On November 8, 1936, the first battalion of these brigades showed up at the front of Madrid, and for two years, they were to turn the tide of the battle.

The Soviet Union's intervention consisted mainly of delivery of war materiel, which was only entrusted to troops solidly under communist control. Some more sophisticated materiel, such as armor and airplanes, remained—as later the missiles in Cuba— in the hands of Russian personnel. The Soviet Embassy in Madrid, later in Valencia, established itself as a kind of second government, which actually directed the Republican war effort.

The Soviet intervention was less addressed to help the republican government to win the war than to establish communist control and to eliminate in the process all non-orthodox factions, such as anarchists and Trotzkyites. These formerly powerful and influential groups in Barcelona were physically liquidated in May 1937 by communist forces under Soviet command.

The danger that these interventions might drag the great powers into the war in Spain seemed imminent at the time. The peace of Europe was, in view of the aggressive attitudes of Italy and Germany, threatened. Italy had conducted its war of conquest in Ethiopia and was threatening France with territorial claims. Germany had unilaterally abrogated the military clauses of the treaty of Versailles and re-occupied the Rhineland. The risk that involvement in Spain might lead to a confrontation of the powers and thence to a general war was ever present, and the governments were well aware of it. France and Britain wanted to avoid war at any cost. The Soviet Union dreaded a war with Germany and had already started to look for avenues leading to a *rapprochement* with Hitler. For Italy, burdened with her African commitments, the fate of Spain was of secondary interest. When France on August 1st, 1936, took the initiative for some agreement on nonintervention, it was favorably received. The agreement was not embodied in a multilateral treaty but in a set of rules, to which the powers individually pledged themselves to adhere. The rules concerned domestic measures designed to prevent arms shipments and the sending of volunteers. They were accepted by France, the United Kingdom, Italy, the Soviet Union, Yugoslavia, Germany, in that order.

The Spanish government (Madrid) protested against these rules for nonintervention. In a letter of August 10, 1936, of the Spanish ambassador in Paris to Yvon Delbos, French Foreign Minister, nonintervention was described as interventionary. The letter said:

> Suspension of exports of arms for the Spanish goverment, in this very moment where it most needs them for reestablishing the normal legal order in its territory, constitutes a very effective intervention in the domestic affairs of Spain.[8]

---

[8] Charles Rousseau, *La Non-Intervention en Espagne* (Paris, 1939), 223.

Neither Italy and Germany, nor France and the Soviet Union seemed really to live up to the rules of nonintervention. Consequently international machinery under the authority of the League of Nations was set up with the mission to enforce the application of the rules. On September 14, 1936, a committee of 27 nations, with a sub-committee of nine nations, composed of Belgium, Czechoslovakia, France, Germany, Italy, Portugal, Sweden, the Soviet Union and the United Kingdom, was set up in London. It was, in the words of one of the foremost students of the Spanish Civil War "to graduate from equivocation to hypocrisy and humiliation."[9] The committee was to provide observers along the land frontiers of Spain and in twelve ports of control, which ships with Spain as their destination were instructed to touch. The land control was effective and almost stopped the flow of volunteers. It was discontinued, however, when in July 1937 Portugal expelled the observers—all British —whereupon France, since the inspection had become one-sided and meaningless, withdrew her permission to the international observer teams to operate from her territory. The inspection of shipping in the ports of control, however, remained in force until the end of the civil war.

The inspection at checkpoints was reinforced by a naval patrol entrusted to France, Great Britain, Italy and Germany. The zones of inspection were based on the principle of antagonism—Germans and Italians preventing foreign ships from reaching the ports of Republican Spain, the French and British preventing ships from reaching the ports of the area held by the Nationalist government of General Franco. Spanish ships were, of course, free from interference, since no blockade was considered which would have implied recognition of belligerency to the two warring factions, which was withheld.

A difficulty resulted from the naval patrol. On May 24, 1937 an Italian warship on patrol was bombarded and on May 29 the German cruiser *Deutschland* was bombed by airplanes of the Republican government, with heavy casualties. In retaliation, Germany revived a typical gunboat policy. On May 31, a naval squadron bombarded the southern town of Almeria, destroying

---

[9] Hugh Thomas, *The Spanish Civil War* (London, 1961), 338.

a number of buildings and killing nineteen people. Soon thereafter Italy and Germany withdrew from the naval patrol.

Not content with the established system for preventing shipments to the Republicans, Italy secretly intervened in the conflict in a new way. "Unidentified" submarines began to attack ships in the Mediterranean headed for government-held ports. These acts of piracy caused international alarm, since they threatened to lead immediately to international war.

An emergency conference was called by the League of Nations. It deliberated from September 10 to 14, 1937, in Nyon, Switzerland. Nine governments of nations bordering the Mediterranean attended. Agreement was reached to the effect that submarines surprised in conducting an unlawful attack would be destroyed. An additional protocol added that the naval patrol, established for the enforcement of the threat and composed of French, British and later Italian warships, would also open fire against agressive airplanes.

Thus a civil war had generated outside intervention, as all prolonged civil wars in an important country invariably will do. This was readily recognized as a danger to international peace; the conflict seemed likely to escalate into major war. The powers basically agreed that the intervention should remain a limited display of force, and cooperated, in spite of their deep antagonisms, in limiting it. The international nonintervention committee in London, with inspection teams, naval patrol and ports of control was a forerunner of later peace-keeping operations as set up by the United Nations. The system was not watertight, and everybody knew it.

The participating nations were determined to circumvent the non-intervention agreements whenever it seemed convenient. Still, it provided them with a useful veil for such activities, and reduced these to a degree where they could, thanks to the face-saving device, be tacitly tolerated by the antagonists.

Chapter VII

Intervention In Our Time – Part One

The Truman Doctrine

After World War II interventions of the police action type by single nations, or by *ad hoc* groups designed to uphold some kind of international legal order, subsided. Problems which otherwise would have called for this age-old method of policing the world were usually now brought to the United Nations and there dealt with after a fashion. What now developed in great style were interventions related to the world conflict termed the "Cold War." Their aim, in most cases, was to support or to establish regimes friendly or favorable to one or the other power group. Even interventions in which only small or medium nations were involved, such as those concerning Yemen (1962) or Cyprus (1964) were, at least indirectly, linked to the contest dominating the world scene.

When the British government notified Washington on February 21, 1947, that beyond the end of the following month it was unable to continue economic, financial and military aid to Greece, which was then involved in a civil war, the first important intervention of the United States of the post war era developed. The decision to come to the aid of Greece was supported by the fact that Turkey, which had also been receiving British assistance, would also require aid and would be in great danger if in Greece the communists were to prevail in the civil war.

The Greek and Turkish situation required action, lest Greece and later perhaps also Turkey be drawn into the orbit of the Soviet Union. It became the point of departure for a new American theory of intervention, a substitute for the earlier set of

109

theories and arguments which had begun in 1823 with the Monroe doctrine and which had passed through the pronouncements of Presidents Theodore Roosevelt and Woodrow Wilson.

The new policy found expression in an address by President Harry S. Truman to a Joint Session of the Congress on March 12, 1947. The key passages read as follows:

> We shall not realize our objectives, however, unless we are willing to help free people to maintain their free institutions and their national integrity against aggressive movements that seek to impose upon them totalitarian regimes. . . Totalitarian regimes imposed on free peoples, by direct or indirect aggression, undermine the foundations of international peace and hence the security of the United States.
>
> . . . . .
>
> I believe that it must be the policy of the United States to support free peoples who are resisting attempted subjugation by armed minorities or by outside pressures. I believe that we must assist free peoples to work out their own destinies in their own way.[1]

The intervention in Greece, thus announced, took the form of massive economic assistance, the delivery of military equipment from World War II stocks, and a mission of military advisors under General James A. Van Fleet. However, it required for the American-assisted Greek army more than two years to bring about the capitulation of the insurgents.

It is evident that the announced intervention in which the United States in 1947 took Great Britain's place in Greece and Turkey, was in reality a measure designed to prevent a decisive shifting of the balance of power in the Eastern Mediterranean area and in the Middle East. The ideological trappings were intended to veil the simple facts of great power policy from the eyes of the American people, who was sentimentally opposed to thinking in such terms.

The President's statement, soon to be termed the Truman Doctrine, was made the *magna charta* of intervention. The reference to "peoples who are resisting attempted subjugation," which qualified the American pledge for support by limiting it to nations who already acted in self defense and thereby manifest-

---

[1] *Documents on American Foreign Policy Relations 1947* (Princeton, N.J.: World Peace Foundation, 1949), 6, 7.

ed their will to remain independent, would soon fall into semi-oblivion. The only yardstick to be used to decide the urgency of intervention for years to come was whether there was a threat that a totalitarian regime might be imposed on a people. From an intelligent method of containing Soviet expansion, the doctrine became a formula for global anti-communism.

The case of Greece was a specific problem growing out of the war and the incapacity of an allied power to go on dealing with this situation. Yet, strangely enough, the President's decision to intervene was clad in words which seemed to infer that the United States would, in the future, support all free peoples who would resist subjugation. In freely attaching the label of a "doctrine" to a foreign policy decision, a tendency manifests itself which, as we will see later in the context of the intervention in Vietnam, is fraught with danger. It prevents the planner and the decision-maker from dealing with a situation or a problem on the merits of the case, by forcing his thinking into the straight jacket of a doctrine.

In his *Memoirs 1925-1950,* the eminent American diplomat and scholar George Kennan reflects on this tendency, in words which merit application to most of the policy decisions with which we are dealing in this book. He writes:

> I have been struck by the congenital aversion of Americans to taking specific decisions on specific problems, and by their persistent urge to seek universal formulae or doctrines in which to clothe and justify particular actions. We obviously dislike to discriminate. We like to find some general governing norm to which, in each instance, appeal can be taken, so that individual decisions may be made not on their particular merits but automatically, depending on whether the circumstances do or do not seem to fit the norm. We like, by the same token, to attribute a universal significance to decisions we have already found it necessary, for limited and parochial reasons, to take.[2]

The ideological trappings of President Truman's action unfortunately would gradually become the basis for many decisions to be taken in the near future.

While it is certain that the support received by the Communists in Greece came from Yugoslavia and Bulgaria rather than from the Soviet Union, whose dictator, Stalin, did not favor

---

[2] George F. Kennan, *Memoirs 1925-1950* (London, 1968), 332.

the operation, it is also certain that the next act of subversion which the world was to witness was entirely directed by Moscow. Czechoslovakia, since 1945 under a popular front government in which the socialists and their democratic allies had a narrow majority, manifested in 1947 its intention to cooperate economically with the West by accepting the invitation contained in the Marshall plan. The Soviet Union ordered Prague to withdraw the acceptance, and the Republic under Benes's weak stewardship duly executed the order.

This was not enough. Moscow decided to intervene in order to establish an all-communist regime. The Ministery of the Interior (and therefore the police) was already in the hands of the Communist Party. In protest against the police pressure exercised on socialist and "bourgeois" parties alike, the non-communist members of the government on February 20, 1948, resigned. A high ranking Soviet representative appeared in Prague and took command of the police through the Ministry of the Interior. Huge communist demonstrations duly impressed Benes. The Foreign Minister, Jan Masaryk, was found dead under a window of his ministry, and the circumstances support the belief that he had been assassinated by Soviet police officers dispatched to Prague. An all-communist government was formed, and the police engaged in a thorough purge of the opposition politicians.

The intervention was effective, masterfully conducted with the help of instruments installed beforehand within the Czechoslovak government, and so swift that practically no resistance was offered within Czechoslovakia or outside. Counter- intervention was not considered on the American side for many reasons. One of them, of overriding importance, was that any step in this direction would have led immediately to a confrontation with the Soviet Union; it was unlikely that such a confrontation would have been kept from exploding into a world-wide conflict. For such a conflict the United States at that time was utterly unprepared. The almost chaotic demobilization of her World War II forces had reflected a traditional American thought: the radical distinction between war and peace.[3] Ac-

---

[3] Urs Schwarz, *American Strategy: A New Perspective* (New York, 1966), 48.

cording to General Marshall, there were, at that time, "1⅓ divisions over the entire United States."[4] Except for her nuclear armaments, the United States was far inferior to the Soviet Union.

Another argument against doing anything could be drawn directly from the wording of President Truman's address; the self-help of the peoples threatened or deprived of their freedom was made a prerequisite of help and intervention. No serious attempt at resistance against the Soviet take-over in Prague had been made.

Korea 1950

When the Japanese war machine collapsed, in 1945, an agreement between Russia and the American General Staff drew a line across the peninsula of Korea along the 38th parallel. North of it Soviet troops would accept surrender of the Japanese forces, south of it the Americans. From this measure of military expediency, and as a result of the impossibility of the Soviet and the American goverments to agree on a single government for the whole of Korea, two distinct governments were gradually set up in each part of the divided country; each began to build its own armed forces.

By one of the tragic misunderstandings of history, the Soviet Union assumed that the United States was not interested in the fate of South Korea and was made to believe that it could unify the country under Communist authority without meeting with American resistance.[5] Therefore, on June 24, 1950, North Korean forces, encouraged and supported by Russia, penetrated across the 38th parallel into South Korea in a major military thrust. President Truman and his advisers immediately realized that the United States had no other choice but to intervene at the side of the threatened government of South Korea.

The diplomatic and military history of the war that ensued has been written in so much detail, that it is not necessary to retrace the events. What is essential for our purpose is that the

---

[4] Samuel P. Huntington, *The Common Defense: Strategic Programs in National Politics* (New York, 1961), 40.

[5] Louis J. Halle, *The Cold War as History* (London, 1967), 206.

United States at once tried to make the intervention a collective one within the framework of the United Nations Charter. Since the Soviet Union, in protest against the Nationalist Chinese government on Formosa occupying the seat of China in the Security Council, had been absent from the Council's meetings since January, the United Nations were, by this coincidence, not prevented from acting. The Council, meeting at the United States' request, and presented with an American draft resolution, resolved on June 25, 1950 that the North Korean attack was a breach of the peace, and called for the cessation of hostilities. The United States invited the members to assist the organization in carrying out the resolution. In the meantime, American forces, hastily organized from the non-combat-ready troops of occupation in South Korea and contingents stationed in Japan, were engaged at the side of the South Korean army. They were vastly outnumbered and soon driven back to the southern tip of the peninsula.

On June 27 the Security Council adopted a new resolution by seven votes to the one of Yugoslavia. It recommended that members of the United Nations furnish such assistance to the Republic of Korea as might be necessary to repel the armed attack and to restore international peace and security. A later resolution requested that members providing military forces make them available to a unified United Nations command. Subsequently, combatant units and supporting elements were provided by sixteen member nations. The bulk of the fight was born by the United States, which also assumed the role of UN military command. The intervention, having gone through critical phases, in the end was successful in a limited way; it ended with the armistice of July 27, 1953.

It was an intervention in the classical form, undertaken in the name of the now existing world security organization and in complete accordance with its aims as set out in the Charter of San Francisco. All the elements were there. The intervention was carried out under the terms of the UN Charter. The combined strength of the forces of the United States and the other members taking part in the operation by far outnumbered the army of North Korea. The deployment of military force in

Korea against the aggressor was a complete departure from the former occupation policy. The aim was limited by the terms of the resolution of the UN Security Council "to repel the armed attack and to restore international peace and security." The objective was to support the existing government in South Korea and to prevent a communist regime under North Korean dominance from being set up.

The action ceased to be an intervention in the strict sense of the word after the victory won by General Douglas MacArthur as a consequence of his landing at Inchon on the west coast of the peninsula on September 15, 1950. The North Korean army was subsequently defeated and practically destroyed. In this situation the American government, fully supported by the allied British government, decided to expand the operations beyond "repelling the attack and restoring peace and security." The opportunity which now offered itself to unite the whole of Korea, which had been divided against the will of its people and against the logic of history, was to be made use of. The General Assembly of the United Nations on October 7 expanded the original mission to the whole of Korea. MacArthur was authorized to continue his advance across the 38th parallel and to occupy Korea up to the Chinese border at the river Yalu. We may say that this decision, in spite of the covering UN resolution, ended intervention and opened the door to a major war designed to effectuate change of the *status quo* by force.

Now, the roles were suddenly reversed. The action of the United Nations had ceased to be an intervention and a new intervenor entered upon the scene. Communist China had viewed the Russian inspired adventure of the North Koreans with great misgivings. It had immediately seen the danger that the Soviet Union, by creating a satellite regime in Korea, was going to win a foothold for the progressive encirclement of China. Now that the Soviet *coup* had utterly failed another, greater danger replaced for the Chinese the first: An American army on the Yalu was looked upon by Peking as an unacceptable threat.

When the movement against the Yalu became a fact on October 1st, 1950, Peking had to make a decision: To intervene or not intervene? The Chinese government seemed to be most reluctant to undertake such a step. It tried to signal Washington that incursions into North Korea by South Korean troops would not be considered a serious problem. But if American troops were to cross the 38th parallel, China would enter the war.[6] The warnings, veiled as they were and almost covered by the noises of violent anti-American outbursts, went unheeded; China acted. MacArthur's armies moved north. On November 6, 1950, Chinese forces, carefully disguised as "volunteers," appeared south of the Yalu.

Chinese intervention was now a fact. It actually took the form of a confrontation, since Peking waited, probably in the hope that negotiations could be engaged. This situation, which might have led to a settlement, if the forces of the United Nations had limited their operations and had conducted them in the form of a confrontation, was not clearly understood by the UN High Command or by General MacArthur. He was convinced that he could win the war within weeks. On November 28, a Chinese offensive broke loose, sweeping MacArthur's forces south and across the 38th parallel. The ensuing war lasted more than two years, and the United Nations and the United States then had to resign themselves to the original aim of the intervention —liberation of South Korea and restoration of peace.

We may say that of two interventions both had been successful—the action to save South Korea on the one hand, the action to prevent the Americans from establishing themselves immediately on the border of China on the other hand.

Wars of National Liberation

Interventions in the domestic affairs of other nations, designed to support friendly governments or to bring into power a government which seems more favorable to the intervening power's interests and concepts, are an almost classical pattern of behavior in our time. In Soviet theory such interventions are based on the principle that "wars of national liberation" have to be supported by the Soviet Union. Marshall Sokolovsky in the volume *Military Strategy* points out:

---

[6] *ibid.*, 222.

The CPSU and the entire Soviet nation have always been the first to oppose any and all aggressive wars (wars between capitalist countries as well as local wars intended to hinder national liberation movements) and they consider it their duty to support the sacred struggle of the oppressed peoples and their just wars of liberation against imperialism.[7]

In the revised edition of Sokolovsky's work the thesis is expanded with the remark that the Soviet Union gives not only ideological and political support but material help as well.[8]

Soviet theory is not very outspoken on this score and hardly goes much farther than to affirm the "sacred duty" to support the national wars of liberation. The Chairman of the Council of Ministers of the Soviet Union in one instance, in December 1963, defended his government's attitude against Chinese criticism, putting in doubt the effectiveness of Soviet interventions in Asia, Africa and Latin America. He declared that the Soviet Union had sent large quantities of arms as a gift to the Algerian patriots. Other Soviet sources point out that armed aid has been given to liberation wars in Indonesia, Yemen and Iraq.[9] The support of the war in Vietnam by sizable shipments of arms and ammunitions to North Vietnam and to the Vietcong has had a decisive influence on the development of the struggle. In the Congo, in 1960, the Soviet Union had sent transport planes, trucks and arms to the government of Patrice Lumumba in the expectation of a civil war which would establish a communist regime.

Within the communist orbit intervention, of course, cannot be based on the concept of wars of liberation. It simply takes, in these cases, the form of action in support of a friendly government or in support of a design to establish such a government. In recent times, it has found its theoretical and ideological expression in the Brezhniev doctrine.

After the death of Stalin, in 1953, the tendency towards a freer conception of communism became particularly strong in Hungary. Mathias Rakosy had re-established a Stalinist government after a two year's interlude of a more "liberal" government

---

[7] Marshall V. D. Sokolovsky, ed., *Military Strategy, Soviet Doctrine and Concepts* (London, 1963), 178.

[8] W. D. Sokolowski, *Militär-Strategie* (Frauenfeld, 1965), 263.

[9] Thomas W. Wolfe, *Sowjetische Militärstrategie* (Köln, 1967), 136.

under Imre Nagy. On July 18, 1956 he was forced to resign, and he was replaced by E. Gero. Encouraged by a strong anti-Stalinist tendency in Poland, a movement of rebellion led by students and young workers developed in Budapest. Gero appealed to Moscow for help, resigned and was replaced, on October 25, 1956, by Imre Nagy. This latter was unable to restrain the revolutionary and nationalistic forces; a national uprising developed which threatened to sweep away the communist regime. For several days, the Soviets conducted deceptive negotiations with the new government about the withdrawal of Soviet forces and the possibility for Hungary to withdraw from the Warsaw Pact. Thereby they gained time to prepare military intervention and to set up a counter-government under Janos Kadar, who would renew the appeal to Moscow; on November 4, 1956 Soviet armies entered Budapest, occupied the capital and brutally suppressed the insurrection. Fighting went on until November 13. Nagy and other leaders of the revolutionary movement were captured by deception, arrested and later executed; the "friendly" regime under Kadar was firmly established. Twelve years later a similar operation was to follow in Czechoslovakia, with far reaching consequences.

Interventions in Africa and the Middle East

Two of the most striking interventions of the sixties in domestic affairs of other nations occured in Africa. Gabon had been part of French Equatorial Africa before it reached independence on August 17, 1960. After less than four years of independence a military revolt broke out. In the early morning of February 18, 1964, the government was overthrown by a group of young officers and President Leon Mba was arrested. In the afternoon of the same day, French troops flown in from Brazzaville in the neighboring Congo-Brazzaville arrived in the capital, Libreville. On the following day a contingent of French forces arrived from Dakar in the Senegal. The rebellion was suppressed and President Mba reinstalled. Paris alleged that the military intervention was conducted under the terms of the treaty for mutual defense of May 17, 1961, and that the step had been taken unilaterally, yet within the treaty, because the president being prisoner had not been able to make the corresponding appeal for help. A few days later, when they discovered in Paris that there was a Vice-President of Gabon, a new and improved version was given to the effect that the Vice-President had invited the French intervention.

The intervention was resented in Africa as being opposed to the principles of nonintervention to which the African states had frequently manifested their absolute adherence. The Secretary General of the *Union Africaine et Malgache,* Germain Mba (no relative of Leon Mba) resigned in protest from his post. He hinted that, since Gabon is a source of manganese and uranium ore, the intervention had served only France's economic interests. France had not found it necessary to intervene in other less interesting instances, as for example when President Fulbert Youlou of Congo-Brazzaville appealed for help, or when President Hubert Maga of Dahomey was overthrown.

On August 28, 1968, President François Tombalbaye, of Chad, another independent republic derived from the former French Equatorial Africa, requested military intervention to suppress a rebellion in the area of Tibesti. The president claimed that he needed this help to suppress the clandestine arms traffic going through that area of the Sahara from the Sudan through the Republic Niger to Nigeria. Following the appeal, the French forces stationed in the capital of Chad, Fort Lamy, were forthwith dispatched to the threatened areas in the east and the north. It soon turned out that they had to face an extended movement of secession opposing the Muslims in the east and the north to the Black African authorities in Fort Lamy, which the French were not able to suppress in spite of their military intervention.[10]

By contrast, when the pro-communist Mali President Modibo Keita was overthrown on November 20, 1968, nobody intervened in his favor.

One of the most active interventionary elements in Africa was Ghana, the former British Gold Coast, under its dynamic president and dictator Kwame Nkrumah. Until he was overthrown by a military *coup* in February 1966, Nkrumah tried to promote revolutionary governments on the pattern of Ghana in

[10] *Le Monde,* Nr. 7642, August 9, 1969 (Paris, 1969).

neighboring states and, by this means, to establish a kind of hegemony in West Africa. He set up in Ghana camps for subversive warfare and tried to infiltrate guerrillas into other countries. His activities were considered by the more moderate African governments to be clearly interventionist, and when the Organization of African Unity (OAU) was founded in 1963 in Addis Ababa, it took a strong anti-interventionist stand. In 1965 it demanded that Ghana discontinue its interventions in other states as a condition for holding the conference of heads of state of OAU at Accra, the capital of Ghana.[11]

The declaration of the United Nations General Assembly of December 21, 1965 solemnly condemned intervention; it came at the height of these activities by Ghana, and to a lesser degree Mali, Guinea, the United Arab Republic, and the Sudan, and it was directed against them.

Another theater for intervention in Africa are the Portuguese possessions of Angola and Mozambique, the Republic of South Africa and Rhodesia. To prepare and conduct interventionary activities, the Organization of African Unity had set up, at its founding meeting in 1963, a Liberation Committee in which nine countries are represented. The base of its activities is Tanzania, its center Dar es Salam.[12] Under this Committee a great number of liberation groups operate; however, they are by no means in agreement as to aims and methods. Their chief activity is to train the Freedom Fighters, many of them recruited among the refugees from the Portuguese possessions or from South Africa. Training for the leaders is provided by Algeria, the United Arab Republic, Cuba and the Soviet Union. Since operations across the borders of the target states have so far been limited to uncoordinated terroristic acts, the liberation "movement" must so far be considered potential, rather than actual intervention.

On June 19, 1961, the sheikdom of Kuwait became an independent nation. The dictator of Iraq, General Kassem, immediately laid claim to the country and reportedly moved troops

---

[11] I. William Zartman, "Intervention Among Developing States," *Journal of International Affairs*, Vol. XXII, No. 2 (New York, 1968), 195.

[12] Donald H. Humphries, *The East African Liberation Movement*, Adelphi Paper No. 16, March 1965 (London, 1965).

towards its borders on the Persian Gulf. On June 30, the ruler of Kuwait asked Saudi Arabia and Great Britain for military assistance. Great Britain assembled land, air and sea forces available in the area, and by July 7th 5,700 British marines and soldiers with two air squadroms were deployed in Kuwait, supported by 40 ships, most of them small ones. Saudi Arabia sent a company of paratroopers. When a month later Kuwait became a member of the Arab League, various Arab governments sent troops, totaling 2,000 to 3,000 men.

The threatened Iraqi invasion never took place, and the government of Kuwait remained in power. Whether the attack had been deterred by the intervention, or whether other domestic reasons prevented General Kassem from proceeding against the sheikdom is still uncertain. The British-Arab intervention had, in its relationship to Iraq, the character of a confrontation. This assertion is strengthened by the fact that the opponents in this particular situation were practically equals as far as power and ability to exercise pressure is concerned. Because of the limited strategic mobility of the British forces, the superior strength of the United Kingdom could not be brought to bear against the smaller Iraqi forces which were close at hand. The absence of any rhetoric of the kind which invariably accompanies American interventions, makes it difficult to discern the real intentions, motivations and the direct effects of each move.

In September, 1962, the ruler of Yemen, an extremely backward country under ancient feudalistic rule, was deposed by the army, or rather the palace guard. The young ruler, who had recently succeeded his father, took to the mountains. The military regime under colonel Abdulla Al-Sallal established itself in Saana and executed many of the former notables. It asked the United Arab Republic for military help. Gamal Abdel Nasser, the ruler of Egypt, sent an expeditionary force of about 40,000 men in support of the military regime which represented modern Arab socialism and nationalism. Saudi Arabia, in turn, supported the side of the forces of the young Imam Saif Al-Badr. The civil war, partly fought by proxy by the UAR and Saudi Arabian forces, dragged on. In February 1963, Washington decided, after considerable disagreement between the Department of State and the

Department of Defense, to encourage a settlement and at the same time to lend Saudi Arabia some support. Under the direction of Robert W. Komer, one of President Kennedy's assistants, negotiations took place and on April 30, 1963, a mutual withdrawal of troops under the supervision of the United Nations was announced. The United States demonstrated their solidarity with Saudi Arabia by conducting joint training exercises with the air force of Saudi Arabia, thus fulfilling the pledge for support given earlier to King Feisal. The operation, jokingly called "Komer's War" by President Kennedy, can not exactly be termed an intervention. It was rather a diplomatic attempt at conciliation, underlined by a very limited show of force.[13] An agreement between the United Arab Republic and Saudi Arabia on August 30, 1967 to end intervention did not end the civil war which continued; the two powers intervening in a much more limited and veiled form.

Friendly Governments

It is a firm belief in America that a clear distinction can be made between "good" and "bad" governments, between "friendly" and "unfriendly" ones. Few realize that in between Jeffersonian democracy and totalitarian rule by a communist or national-socialist dictatorship there is a wide variety of alternative methods to govern nations. Few seem to realize that "good" and "bad," moral categories, applied in a simplified and emotional way, are not the categories on which a world power really bases her policy decisions. Few realize that the relationship to America is not the main concern of every government, and that many nations do not orient their course on the shining star of friendly relations to Washington. This is not altogether the American's fault, since the eagerness to partake of the wealth streaming out of the horn of plenty of foreign aid has tempted many statesmen and politicians all over the world to feign excessive concern for American opinion and benevolence.

In a mood to over-compensate the former isolationism, the belief spread in the United States that every event in the world

---

[13] Charles W. Koburger, "Komer's War. The Indirect Strategy in Action." *Military Review*, Vol. 49, No. 8, August 1969 (Fort Leavenworth, Kansas, 1969), 18.

directly affected America's peace and security. Serious and experienced men such as a professor at Harvard Law School and former Deputy Assistant Secretary of Defense, were able to make the following statement:

> The greatest threat to the security of the United States is the breakdown of public order. Public order tends to break down primarily in the less developed parts of the world, and usually for reasons not associated with the expansionist drive of Communist states or parties.[14]

The resulting misconception has created an interventionist mood in America, not unlike the one which existed in the Nineteenth and early Twentieth centuries with regard to Latin America. While the interventions of the earlier period were oriented towards the capability of the target societies to maintain peace and order and to respect and protect foreign interests, the new series of interventions has been devoted to a more ambitious goal: to favor governments which either corresponded to American traditional ideals and which would maintain public order (and hence promote the security of the United States) or which, if this was not possible, would at least be anti-communist. There is a voluminous literature, ranging from scholarly writing to science fiction, which deals with interventions in support of friendly governments or designed to overthrow those of a less friendly character. The administration of foreign aid quite openly professes such aims; the Congress has insisted time and again that support of friendly governments has to be the aim of economic, technological and military assistance to foreign countries and indulges in exaggerated views of the effectiveness of such help. Secretary of Defense Robert McNamara coined the word "security is development." The Central Intelligence Agency (CIA) is credited with a wide range of secret activities and almost superhuman cunning in doing and undoing governments.

Since America is so eager to influence the way in which other nations should be governed, a paradoxical situation develops. Trusting that aid and assistance are an effective method of intervention which influences another nation's choice, preference is given to assistance to unfriendly governments rather than

---

[14] Adam Yarmolinsky, "American Foreign Policy and the Decision to Intervene," *Journal of International Affairs, loc. cit.,* 235.

to friendly ones. Naturally, interest of the giver concentrates on the recipient of gifts. This creates the harmful impression and the widely held view that the United States prefers to help her enemies and tends to neglect her friends.

Eagerness to intervene also makes the United States vulnerable to manipulation by foreign powers. With threats to go right or left, even small nations, provided their government has the necessary politico-psychological insight, ruthlessness and cunning, can easily influence policy decisions in Washington.

It was inevitable that interventionistic enthusiasm was followed, especially after the Vietnam experience, by some reaction and second thoughts. In an article, *To Intervene or not to Intervene,* Hans J. Morgenthau comes to the conclusion that—

> We have come to overrate enormously what a nation can do for another nation by intervening in its affairs—even with the latter's consent.[15]

Even more bluntly, Edwin O. Reischauer, former ambassador in Japan, wrote:

> Any regime that is not strong enough to defend itself against its internal enemies probably could not be defended by us either and may not be worth defending anyway.[16].

It would be tedious to enumerate all the known and half-known instances in which very limited interventions promoting "good" or "friendly" governments have taken place. A few examples may suffice.

In June 1954 the government of Guatemala, headed by General Jacobo Arbenz was overthrown by a military revolt, disguised as an invasion from Honduras. The United States had earlier tried to prevent arms imports from Eastern Europe to the Arbenz government, and Secretary of State John Foster Dulles, in March, 1954, at the OAS Conference in Caracas, had tried to mobilize Latin American opinion against Guatemala. The United States, at the same time, clandestinely provided arms to the revolutionaries and encouraged them.

---

[15] Hans. J. Morgenthau, "To Intervene or Not to Intervene," *Foreign Affairs,* Vol. 45, No. 3, April 1967 (New York: The Council on Foreign Relations, 1967), 436.

[16] Quoted by Robert E. Osgood, *cf.* note 6 Chapter VIII.

In 1955 an invasion of Costa Rica by Nicaraguan forces was repelled with the help of aircraft supplied by the United States to the government of Costa Rica. This action, which could be simply viewed as selling airplanes to an embattled government, would not necessarily appear as an intervention, had it not been presented, expressly, as a collective action in defense of the peace of the Americas, an action undertaken in response to an appeal of Costa Rica to the Organization of American States.

An American scholar, Richard J. Barnet, who had been for many years and in various capacities in the service of the Government of the United States, gives a case history of interventions, especially American interventions.[17] He not only deals with the more spectacular cases of intervention but also uncovers the role the Central Intelligence Agency and other government agencies had or allegedly had in revolutionary movements such as in Egypt when the monarchy was overthrown in 1952, in Bolivia (1952), in Lebanon (1952), in Iran, when the Mossadeq government was ousted (1953), in the revolt originating in Sumatra against the Indonesian government of Sukarno (1957), in Cuba, in Santo Domingo, and in British Guiana against the Jagan government (1961). The book is biased in favor of change and of revolution as such, as a means of change "if there is nothing better"[18] and is a passionate plea against an imperialistic outlook and a militaristic analysis of the world environment. This sheds doubt on the factual accuracy of many of its statements, but does not diminish the importance of the book as a powerful critic of the interventionary trends existing in United States foreign policy.

The Eisenhower Doctrine

President Eisenhower's—or rather Secretary of State John Foster Dulles's—policy in the Middle East culminated, in 1955, in the conclusion of the Baghdad pact which brought together the strange group Great Britain, Turkey, Iraq, Iran and Pakistan. The treaty seemed to link the North Atlantic Pact and the South

---

[17] Richard J. Barnet, *Intervention and Revolution, The United States in the Third World* (New York, 1968).
[18] *ibid.,* 284.

East Asia Treaty by members like Britain, Turkey and Pakistan. The pact system was the expression of Dulles's firm belief, almost a fixed idea, that no nation could protect itself from the onslaught of Soviet imperialism unless it joined an alliance. The pact could not prevent Soviet influence from growing among the Arabs and it did not prevent the growing movement of subversion directed against conservative governments in Saudi Arabia, Lebanon, Iraq, Jordan, Kuwait and Yemen by Gamal Abdel Nasser's Egypt. The confrontation over Suez, in which the United States had sided with the Arabs and the Soviet Union against the Western powers, did not improve the situation. Subversion was rampant throughout the area. The governments which tried to resist Egyptian subversion and the appeal of the Soviet Union had to be supported. The Eisenhower government concluded that it might be forced to intervene in the Middle East, and accordingly laid the groundwork for such an operation. By announcing its determination, it was hoped, the governments of countries such as Lebanon, Jordan, Iraq, Saudi Arabia, Kuwait, Yemen, which felt threatened, would be encouraged.

On March 9, 1957, a joint resolution was adopted by the Congress of the United States, which had been formulated after two months of painful negotiations with congressional leaders. The pronouncement was termed *Joint Resolution to Promote Peace and Stability in the Middle East*. It went beyond the Truman doctrine, which had referred to the duty to support free peoples who are resisting attempted subjugation by armed minorities or by outside pressures. The joint resolution, to which the label "the Eisenhower Doctrine" soon was to be attached, threw the arms wide open by expressly encouraging governments to invite armed intervention by the United States. On the other hand, it expressed legalistic timidity by limiting the intention to intervene to the narrow field of armed aggression from a country "controlled by international communism"—whatever this may mean—another fixed idea of Secretary Dulles. The decisive Section 2 of the resolution reads as follows:

> The President is authorized to undertake, in the general area of the Middle East, military assistance programs with any nation or group of nations of that area desiring such assistance. Furthermore, the United States regards as vital to the national interest and world

peace the preservation of the independence and integrity of the nations of the Middle East. To this end, if the President determines the necessity thereof, the United States is prepared to use armed force to assist any such nation or group of nations requesting assistance against armed aggression from any country controlled by international communism: *Provided,* that such employment shall be consonant with the treaty obligations of the United States and with the Constitution of the United States.[19]

On February 1st, 1958, Egypt and Syria joined in the United Arab Republic. In the process, Syria became as "the Syrian Province" part of Egypt and under its ruler, Abdel Nasser. As a counter move, a treaty of confederation was concluded between Iraq and Jordan. This, however, inflamed resistance against the King of Jordan and the dictatorial regime of Nuri-es-Said in Iraq. On July 14, 1958, in Baghdad, the government was overthrown in a bloody military *coup,* and the dictator and the King, Faisal II, were assassinated.

On May 22, 1958, Lebanon had complained to the Security Council of the United Nations that agents were being infiltrated into the country from Egypt and Syria and that arms were being supplied from Syria to the opponents of the government, with the object to bring about the absorption of Lebanon into the United Arab Republic. By the end of June the situation in Lebanon had developed into one of civil war, where different pro-and anti-UAR-factions fought for power and the army limited itself to the physical protection of the established government. The United Nations, based upon a resolution proposed by Sweden on June 11, had sent observation groups to the border of Syria; these limited themselves to the task of not finding any proof for an infiltration of agents or armed personnel.

The day of the *coup* in Baghdad, the Chamoun government in Lebanon repeated its earlier appeals to the United States to intervene in its favor under the terms of the Eisenhower Doctrine in order to prevent a take-over by the pro-Egyptian factions. A similar appeal was made to London by King Hussein of Jordan, his government and the Jordanian National Assembly. There had been, for Washington, plenty of time to observe the deterioration of the situation and for consulting with the United Kingdom.

[19] *Documents on American Foreign Relations 1957* (Princeton, N.J.: World Peace Foundation, 1957), 206.

On July 15 and 16 the US Sixth Fleet landed three battalion landing teams near Beirut on the shores of Lebanon; the landing was unopposed. On July 17 the United Kingdom sent a force of paratroopers to Jordan. Ten days later, by air and sea transport, a total of 6,000 U.S. marines and 8,000 soldiers had been brought to Lebanon.[20] The presence of American forces soon brought about a cease-fire in the civil war. A diplomatic emissary, Robert Murphy, secured an agreement between the Lebanese army command, which had been deeply involved in the crisis, and some of the opposition groups. On July 31, the Lebanese parliament elected General Chehab, the Army commander, to succeed President Chamoun.

On the very day of the troop landings in Lebanon the American government addressed itself to the Security Council of the United Nations to explain the nature of the intervention. The British government took similar action. The two governments moved that the Security Council entrust the protection of the integrity and security of the Middle Eastern nations to a UN security force. Both were eager to internationalize the problem and to disengage themselves as soon as possible from their commitment. There was some fear that the Soviet Union would support the United Arab Republic and that a serious confrontation might develop. Moscow, however, did not go beyond a proposal, contained in a letter of July 20 to the heads of government of the United States, the United Kingdom, France and India, to meet two days later in Geneva. The replies were inconclusive. The Soviet Union therefore moved in the Security Council on August 7 that an emergency session of the General Assembly be called. The Session took place from August 8 to 21, 1958 in New York. On its last day, it adopted a resolution proposed by ten Arab nations, calling upon the members of the United Nations to act in accordance with the principles of mutual respect for each other's territorial integrity and sovereignty, the principles of nonagression and the principles of strict noninterference in each other's internal affairs.[22] The Secretary General was to make ar-

---

[20] Neville Brown, *Strategic Mobility* (London, 1963), 73.

[21] General Assembly Resolution 1237 (ES-III) *United Nations Yearbook 1958*, 46.

rangements which would uphold the principles of the Charter in relation to Lebanon and Jordan and which would facilitate the withdrawal of the foreign troops. On October 25 the American troops were withdrawn from Lebanon and on November 2 the British troops left Jordan. The two Middle Eastern countries remained independent.

In the debates at the United Nations the two interventions were presented by the United States and Britain as abstract motions in the name of the security of sovereign nations against outside interference and subversion fostered by foreign countries. This had actually been the outward mechanism of the double intervention. Its real role in the international environment, however, had been to prevent a significant alteration in the balance of power.

Rome and Santo Domingo

One of the far reaching and delayed effects of the Hungarian revolution of 1956 was the break between the Italian Socialist Party led by Pietro Nenni and the Communist Party. In the late fifties in Rome there had, consequently, been some maneuvering of the left wing of the Christian Democrats toward a broader coalition government, excluding the Right and including instead the Social-Democrats, with the support of Nenni's Socialists—the *apertura a sinistra*. In Eisenhower's time the United States had—one of their subtle interventions—opposed the project. After the change of the administration early in 1961 the advisers in the White House began to reverse the course. In a revealing chapter in his book *A Thousand Days,* Arthur M. Schlesinger, Jr.[22] gives an account of moves undertaken in 1963 by forces in Washington, supported by the Vatican, to bring about a change in Rome. They consisted of informing the leaders of the center and left parties in Rome that the United States would look favorably upon an opening to the left. It is interesting to note how the intellectuals in the White House, especially Schlesinger and the already mentioned Robert Komer, thought of a union between socialists and left wing

---

[22] Arthur M. Schlesinger Jr., *A Thousand Days* (London, 1965), 750.

catholics as a model for Germany, France and—later, after they would hopefully have overthrown General Franco,—Spain. It is interesting that they felt responsible for the best composition of future European governments, which in their view seemed to be unaware of the signs of the times and unable to judge for themselves what policy suited them best. It is not less interesting to read the argument which the Department of State used, at the end of 1962, against the *apertura*: When the United States of America permitted it, it would encourage Moscow to doubt the West's determination. In December 1963 the operation—supported by the friendly gestures vis-a-vis the left made by the Catholic church under Pope John XXIII—was successful. Nenni entered the Italian government. The American intervention ushered in years of instability for Italy.

The Dominican Republic has been, for a hundred years, a place of frequent interventions by the United States of America. If ever intervention was warranted, it was here, in view of the absolutely chaotic political life of the little Republic, its tradition of violence, bloodshed and the total lack of security for Dominicans and foreigners alike.

On April 24, 1965, a new revolt broke out in the capital city, Santo Domingo, against the military dictatorship which had been set up about two years earlier after the assassination of the dictator Rafael Trujillo in May 1961. The American Embassy, alarmed by the violent character of the uprising and under the influence of information of doubtful value, concluded that a communist take-over was threatening and accordingly reported to Washington. Afraid that "another Cuba" was going to emerge and under the pressure of reports of severe fighting and bloodshed, President Lyndon B. Johnson, on April 28, 1965 ordered the Marines, which had been kept in readiness, to land.

The reaction in Latin America and the whole world, highly sensitized by the war in Vietnam, was one of universal indignation against the intervention. The United States at once moved to internationalize the intervention and to extricate themselves from the ill-considered commitment. The Council of the Organization of American States immediately met and on May 1st dispatched a special committee to Santo Domingo, which suc-

ceeded in establishing a kind of truce between the warring factions. The OAS requested the members to send troops to the
Dominican Republic. On May 22, 1965 these were placed under
unified command as an Inter-American Peace Force, headed by
a Brazilian commander and a United States deputy commander.
On August 31, 1965, an *Act of Dominican Reconciliation* was
signed under the auspices of the Organization of American
States; the foreign troops were gradually withdrawn.

The Dominican intervention is of great interest. It was begun
under the impact of a typical impulse—the impulse to protect a
"friendly government" and to prevent a change which, according to cold war parlance, presented the risk of a "communist
takeover." As it soon turned out, the communist danger could
not be proved, and the situation created by the landing of troops
was morally so damaging that internationalization was immediately sought and achieved.

The Latin American nations, it will be noted, did not
hesitate to intervene in turn, since it could be done collectively,
and the Dominicans failed to object to such intervention, as soon
as it was transferred from the individual responsibility of the
United States to the collective responsibility of the Organization
of American States.

In the middle of the Dominican turmoil, on May 28, 1965
President Lyndon B. Johnson, speaking at Baylor University,
gave expression to the principle of collective action—he had
neglected it a month earlier—and gave a new touch to the policy
of favoring friendly governments. The old concept that a "communist takeover" must be resisted is now limited to the Western
Hemisphere. The intervention, in this case will be collectively
conducted by the OAS. And then the President added another
motivation for future intervention: Those who maintain a feudal
system which denies social justice and economic progress will
be opposed. The intervention will be collective intervention by
the OAS. Johnson said:

> In times past large nations have used their power to impose their
> will on smaller nations. Today we have placed our forces at the
> disposition of the nations of this hemisphere to assure the peoples
> of those nations the right to exercise their own will in Freedom.

In accordance with the resolution of the 8th meeting of the ministers at Punta del Este, we will join with the other OAS nations in opposing a communist takeover in this hemisphere.

And in accordance with the charter of Punta del Este, we will join with other OAS nations in pressing for change among those who would maintain a feudal system—a feudal system that denies social justice and economic progress to the ordinary peoples of this hemisphere.

We want for the peoples of this hemisphere only what they want for themselves—liberty, justice, dignity, a better life for all.[23]

---

[23] *Documents on American Foreign Relations 1965*, 261.

Chapter VIII

Intervention In Our Time – Part Two

Intervention Within Confrontation

Three scenarios of modern intervention have already been mentioned in the chapter on confrontation because they were closely woven into three of the most spectacular confrontations of our time: Suez, the Congo, Cyprus.

The French and British operation against Egypt in 1956, preceded by an attack by Israel, was an intervention of the nineteenth century style. It was primarily designed to recover the Suez Canal, which had been nationalized in an unilateral act by Egypt. This was the paramount British interest. To destroy at its source the aid, comfort, encouragement and direction of the rebellion in Algeria, which had started in 1954 and which depended greatly on Egypt was the most pressing motivation for France. This great power intervention led immediately to a collective intervention by the United Nations.

The Franco-British operation failed because it had been started too late and conducted too slowly, because the command structure and communications system of the joint French-British forces was inefficient, and because Israel had been encouraged to take part in the attack and was then prevented from carrying through its part.[1] In the ensuing confrontation with the Soviet Union, the two intervenors were forced to yield because the United States sided with the Soviet Union in opposing France and Britain. The nuclear threat, combined with powerful diplomatic and political action in an emergency special session of the General Assembly of the United Nations which convened on October 31, 1956 were the decisive factors.

---

[1] General Beaufre, *Die Suez-Expedition, Analyse eines verlorenen Sieges* (Berlin, 1968), 182.

The cease-fire of November 6, 1956, was the direct result of a highly successful intervention by the United Nations. When Lester Pearson of Canada made the proposal in the General Assembly on November 2 that a United Nations peace force should be placed at the Suez Canal, four countries at once offered troops, and within a few days the pledges rose to twenty-four. Offers of troops were finally accepted from Brazil, Canada, Colombia, Denmark, Finland, India, Indonesia, Norway, Sweden and Yugoslavia. On November 15, Swiss aircraft chartered by the Swiss government began to land the main force after advance parties of the new United Nations Emergency Force (UNEF) had been installed.[2] The international intervention gave overwhelming expression of the state of international opinion; it was the pressure of this opinion, rather than nuclear threats proffered by Moscow, which moved France and Britain to discontinue the operation.

It is highly significant that two European powers with well-trained and relatively well-equipped forces at their disposal, and which had a valid legal title to defend against an internationally unlawful act—the seizure of the Suez Canal against a series of treaty obligations freely entered into by Egypt—completely failed in their attempt. The intervention had been directed against a weak and unstable regime with a poorly trained army. However, in the then-existing political environment, intervention became unfeasible. The Suez crisis, with the ensuing defeat of France and Britain, is to be considered as a turning point in the history of intervention.

The Congo crisis of 1960 gave rise to the second full scale intervention of the United Nations. It differed from the first intervention of similar magnitude, the one in Korea, 1950 to 1953, insofar as it was conducted in an infinitely more complicated international environment; on the other hand it was similar, since it included extensive use of military force.

On July 12, 1960, the President of the new Republic of the Congo jointly with his Prime Minister Patrice Lumumba, addressed a telegram to the Secretary General of the United Nations; in it he requested the military assistance of the world organization against "external aggression" and against the seces-

---

[2] Neville Brown, *Strategic Mobility* (London, 1963), 68.

sion of the Katanga province. By "external aggression" the Congolese leaders referred to the intervention by Belgian forces, which were brought from Europe into the Congo after the mutiny of the *force publique,* in order to protect the life and the property of foreigners, who actually were in extreme danger.

Following proposals of the Secretary General, the Security Council of the United Nations on July 14, 1960 adopted a resolution calling upon Belgium to withdraw its troops. At the same time, it instructed the Secretary General to give the Congolese Government military and technical aid until its own security forces could restore peace and order. Immediately, the Secretary General set up an organization, *Operation des Nations Unies au Congo,* (ONUC). One branch was designed to help the civilian administration of the new Republic, the other to organize a military force, composed of contingents from countries other than the great powers and world powers.

The Secretary General of the United Nations, Dag Hammarskjöld, immediately turned to two African nations, Ethiopia and Tunisia, who were ready to comply; Tunisia with the proviso that Morocco would also send troops. Morocco agreed, and on July 18 contingents from three countries were airlifted to Leopoldville by the United States Air Force. Ghana spontaneously sent an advance party of her army. A week later the Swedish battalion serving under the United Nations in the Gaza strip was airlifted to the Congo. During the three following days forces from Ghana and an Irish battalion of volunteers arrived. Political rivalries of course soon came to play a role; when the United Arab Republic offered troops, the Sudan insisted that it also would send some. The same occurred with India and Pakistan. In September 1960 the ONUC consisted of nearly 20,000 men. By this time, all the Belgian forces had been withdrawn. For civilian operations, the United Nations had 120 experts at their disposal.[3]

When Colonel Mobutu had seized power in Leopoldville on September 13, 1960, four opposing Congolese groups, each with an army of its own, for almost a year struggled for power. The United Nations, therefore, had to cooperate with the local au-

---

[3] *ibid.,* 80.

thorities which happened to be in power in each area. Their mission consisted in preventing armed clashes, disarming certain groups, protecting the people, their property, and the politicians threatened by the other faction. In retrospect, this operation may be termed very successful, since it finally resulted in setting up a central government on August 2, 1961, and since enough of the few available leaders had survived the internecine struggle.

A special phase of the international intervention in the Congolese affairs was the result of the secession of the Katanga province. After independence, Katanga, under the leadership of Moise Tshombe, powerfully backed by the enormous European industrial interests existing in this most valuable area of the Congo, declared its independence. The central government under Lumumba at once requested the United Nations to recapture the province by armed force. Hammarskjöld refused to do so. Instead, by dealing directly with the Belgian government and, on the spot, with the authorities of Katanga, he negotiated the peaceful replacement of Belgian forces by the troops of the United Nations.

The presence of ONUC did not prevent the arrival of great numbers of foreign advisers for the provincial government under Tshombe and numbers of foreign mercenaries who were to serve in the Katanga *gendarmerie*. It was a clandestine operation, conducted by western interests, very similar to the one of the Soviets at the beginning of the Congo crises. The Security Council therefore urged, on February 21, 1961, the evacuation of all foreign personnel and authorized the use of force as a last resort to prevent civil war. When finally, in August, a central national government was formed at Leopoldville, it opened negotiations with Tshombe in the hope of fully reintegrating Katanga and ending its secession. When these negotiations failed—they were dramatic, because Tshombe was arrested when he did not agree —the central government asked the ONUC's help for the evacuation of the mercenaries serving in the Katanga forces.

In accepting this task, the intervention of the United Nations entered upon a new phase. Under the resolution of the Security Council of August 9, 1960, the United Nations had stated that they and their security forces "will not be a party to or in any way intervene in or be used to influence the outcome of any internal conflict, constitutional or otherwise." A year after this resolution had been adopted, the United Nations, under the pressure of the African, Asian and Communist members, had to go much further and to intervene on behalf of the central government in the domestic conflict brought about by the attitude of the Katanga authorities—whoever they may have been at that time.

On August 28, 1961, ONUC forces in South Katanga surrounded the headquarters of the *gendarmerie*, occupied the Elisabethville radio station and succeeded in rounding up, without firing a shot, a large proportion of the mercenaries. They were deported. Many, however, had escaped. The ONUC tried to repeat the operation on September 13, but this time the *gendarmerie* was warned and resisted. In order to negotiate a cease fire, Secretary General Hammarskjöld rushed to the scene. He planned to meet Tshombe on neutral ground in Ndola in Northern Rhodesia. On September 18 on a flight to the appointment he and his party found death together in an air crash. Other officers of the United Nations finally succeeded in concluding a cease fire with Tshombe. Yet, the conflict continued, and increased pressure was exercised against ONUC. The operations of the Katanga forces mainly consisted in setting up road blocks and to hinder, by the most diverse methods, the movements of the United Nations forces, thereby making them ineffective. In a resolution of November 24 the Security Council expressly authorized the use of force to eliminate mercenaries. To gain freedom of maneuver the United Nations forces, on December 5, 1961, took action against the opponents, and some fighting ensued until December 19. By that time ONUC could move in the province without impediment. The provincial authorities resumed negotiations with the central government, under the auspices of the United Nations, which included protection of the Katanga negotiators from arrest, a practice current in the Congo.

Since no agreement could be reached by the Congolese leaders, the United Nations presented a "Plan of National Reconciliation" in August 1962. This provided for a federal system, in which Katanga would keep some autonomy and could dispose of part of its revenue. This plan was accepted yet not implemented by Katanga. On December 13, 1962, the Secretary General of the UN invited several member states to use economic pressure on Katanga in order to obtain compliance. In reply, the United Nations forces were again attacked by the *gendarmerie*. On December 28, 1962, the United Nations forces began to remove all the road blocks. They found little resistance. On January 13, 1963, the Katanga government finally agreed to cooperate with ONUC and to end the secession; towards the end of January a representative of the central government took up residence in Elisabethville.

This international intervention represents another turning point. An operation originally designed to preserve order and security and to prevent atrocities,—in essence a humanitarian intervention—an operation which was to leave it entirely to the target society to choose its system of government and to select its leaders, was forced by events to outgrow its original purpose. The intervenor had to take sides for one of two conflicting political concepts—in this case the preservation of national integrity within the borders of the former colonial empire. It had to engage in military operations to disarm one faction in the civil war, thus taking sides for the other faction. It had to impose a constitutional project on the intervened country.

All this was done by the United Nations, and the result was not altogether negative, since some kind of order was established and a central government authority permitted gradually to develop.

Cyprus became, in the early fifties, a trouble spot which led, as we have seen, to serious confrontations between Turkey and Greece—the world powers remaining in the background. In spite of the agreements reached in 1958 and 1959 in Zurich and London on the future of the island and its inhabitants, including full independence, peace and stability were not achieved for the new nation. The conflict between the Greek majority and the Turkish minority led in December 1963 to severe fighting. The three guaranteeing powers under the treaty of guarantee of 1959, Great Britain, Greece and Turkey, met in London. Since the three were also signatories of the North Atlantic Treaty, they agreed to offer to send a NATO peace force to Cyprus. The offer was rejected by the Cypriote government under Archbishop Makarios.

The Security Council of the United Nations, following an appeal by Cyprus, on March 4, 1964, resolved to send a peace force to Cyprus. It was to be made up of troops from Australia, Austria, Canada, Denmark, Finland, Great Britain, Ireland, New Zealand and Sweden, under an Indian general. The crisis moved faster than the world organization. On March 13, Turkey addressed an ultimatum to the Makarios government, threatening with invasion. The Security Council answered with a resolution asking the members of the United Nations to abstain from military threats. An advance party of UNFICYP, a few Canadian officers and men, were rushed to the island. This permitted Turkey to withdraw her ultimatum without loss of face. The force, the establishment of which had been delayed by the problem of its financing, became operative on March, 27.

UNFICYP could not prevent violence between the two ethnic communities, which were supported by Greece and Turkey, respectively. However, for more than three years, it maintained a delicate balance and helped to gain time for negotiations and mediation.

The intervention corresponded in its method and in the instructions, given by the Security Council to the Security force, to the first phase of the Congo intervention. In an *aide memoire* of April 10, 1964, Secretary General U Thant carefully interpreted the powers given the force by the Security Council. He pointed out:

> The troops of the Force carry arms which, however, are to be employed only for self-defense, should this become necessary in the discharge of its function, in the interest of preserving international peace and security, of seeking to prevent a recurrence of fighting, and contributing to the maintenance and restoration of law and order and a return to normal conditions. The personnel of the Force must act with restraint and with complete impartiality towards the members of the Greek and Turkish Cypriote communities.[4]

---

[4] Finn Seyersted, *United Nations Forces in the Law of Peace and War* (Leyden, 1966), 83.

The document proceeds by giving detailed instructions as to what is to be understood by self-defense.

Contrary to the evolution in the Congo, where ONUC, the United Nations army was, in a second phase, instructed to use force in order to end the secession of Katanga, in Cyprus the troops were never allowed to take sides in the civil war. This, of course, is nothing but a reflection of the international environment and the state of the enveloping confrontation, of which the intervention of the United Nations was a part. In the Congo, overwhelming pressure by the Afro-Asian countries, the Soviet Union and other communist nations was exercised in order to bring Katanga under Leopoldville's authority. The Secretary General of the UN—and the United States—could not resist such pressure. In Cyprus, the developing world was not really interested in the issue, and the two super powers felt divided loyalties towards the factions on Cyprus. The United States had to avoid, if possible, antagonizing either one of its two allies, Turkey and Greece. The Soviet Union tried to avoid a conflict with Makarios, whose anti-western attitude was valuable to her; at the same time the Kremlin had initiated a *rapprochement* with Turkey which seemed promising. For the two powers it would have been impossible to take sides, and therefore the United Nations force remained a neutral intervenor-conciliator.

Vietnam

The Vietnam war, the origins of which go back to the compromise reached in the conference of Geneva in 1954, provides an example of how technical, economic and military aid, combined with political advice, all relatively peaceful forms of intervention directed at establishing a friendly regime, may degenerate into military intervention, and the intervention deblinded to the realities by its own sense of mission and by an erroneous assessment of the power structures in the target society, engages in an intervention which goes much further than originally contemplated. This extension eventually brings a government into opposition not only to its enemies, but to its own public opinion, its friends, the intervened nation, and to its own interests.

The action carried to South Vietnam by the United States of America differs from any other intervention we have examined so far. What were the essentials of interventions? A short recapitulation will help to discover the fundamental differences and also some similarities between other interventions and the one in Vietnam.

The intervention in the Greek Civil war in 1947 was directed to a conflict which had started earlier, and for the outcome of which responsibility had been tossed, so to say, by an allied power to the United States. In view of the importance of the outcome to the balance of power, this responsibility was accepted.

The intervention in Korea in 1950 was primarily conceived as protection of a nation against an attack. It was synonymous with taking sides in an existing war, and it was supported by a collectivity of nations.

The intervention of the Soviet Union in Hungary in 1956 was directed against a government which had decided to terminate a treaty and alliance engagements entered into by its predecessor. It re-established political dominance against a movement of rebellion and redressed the balance of power.

The intervention by France and Great Britain in Egypt in 1956 was an operation designed to restore a formerly held power position and to overthrow and replace a regime which had become, in the eyes of the intervening powers, untrustworthy and even harmful and dangerous for their interests.

The intervention of the United States in Lebanon in 1958 came in response to an appeal by a government threatened to be overthrown by its enemies, foreign and domestic.

The intervention by Great Britain and the Arab League in Kuwait in 1964 was designed to uphold the independence of a little nation against one of its neighbors, and with its independence also to protect the oil interests existing in that country.

The opposing interventions by the United Arab Republic and by Saudi Arabia in Yemen in 1965 tried to influence the outcome of an existing civil war and, by its outcome, to attract the country into one's own power orbit.

The intervention of the United States in the Dominican Republic in 1965 equally tried to influence the outcome of a civil war, which had already broken out.

Vietnam was different. Here a country, emerging from a century of colonial dependence, was divided by an armistice into two halves which were foreordained to become bitter antagonists. The United States, which was not a party to these agreements, promised economic aid, political advice and assistance in training an army, including the supply of arms to the southern half, South Vietnam. Intervention was not carried knowingly into an existing conflict, as in all the other cases, but it rather grew together with and parallel to a new, slowly developing crisis.

The Americans probably could have avoided this growing entanglement had they applied the knowledge they had. In the ten years which had elapsed since the end of World War II, America had witnessed the unhappy evolution of Vietnam: liberation from the Japanese occupation by the Allies in union with nationalistic forces, including communists; and the establishment of an independent state under Ho Chi Minh and his Vietminh within the French Union. Soon, in November, 1946 there followed an open clash between Ho Chi Minh and the French; answered by the establishment of the Bao Dai regime over the whole of Indochina by France, and the extended warfare between the French and the Vietminh forces.

In 1950, after the final collapse of the regime of Chiang Kai-shek in China, America was gripped by the not entirely rational desire to protect the Chiang Kai-shek regime in Formosa, to defend Korea, and to contain the Soviet Union in Europe within the borders Moscow had conquered in the war. The sweeping statement that "we must assist free peoples to work out their own destinies in their own way" as announced in the Truman doctrine, contributed to a colossal picture of a crusade against the solid antagonistic forces of "Soviet-Chinese Communism."

The American attitude had been, throughout these years, and even much earlier under the administration of Franklin D. Roosevelt, one of favoring independence of Indochina against French colonial rule. This course was reversed under the impulse of the anticommunist complex. In spite of its familiarity with all the weaknesses of the French position and in spite of its basic opposition to French policy, the Truman administration's Secretary of State Dean Acheson concluded, as early as May, 8, 1950, an agreement with Paris which pledged American support in the war against the Vietminh. The French position collapsed in 1954, not without an agonizing search in Washington for a method to salvage it. Military intervention, including nuclear strikes, was considered as a possibility, and averted only by a miracle.

After the division of the country was decided upon in Geneva in 1954, the United States, which did not feel bound by the armistice agreements to which it was not a party, almost enthusiastically tried to take the place of the departed French, but in the traditional spirit of anti-colonialism. The United States considered it a duty to promote in South Vietnam an independent, healthy, prosperous, democratic, non-communist Asian state. At the same time it saw its chance to build a "bulwark against communism"—in short, a showpiece for the world to see. That the war-torn, corrupt and rotten Indochina would never serve as a basis for such an ambitious project did not seem to occur to the planners and builders.

The effort undertaken was as confused as the forces which stood behind it were varied. Liberal intellectuals, the military, passionate anti-communists, idealists with a sense of mission, strong Catholic influences, all wanted to contribute to the nation-building on the quicksands of South East Asia. As the central figure of the new nation a man with a solid anti-French, anti-Japanese, anti-communist and nationalistic reputation was selected, Ngo Dinh Diem, a devout Catholic from one of the great families of the country. Once this regime was in power, it was not willing to accept the risk of the general elections, which, according to the armistice agreement concluded in Geneva in 1954, were to be held not later than 1956, as a step towards the reunification of the two Vietnams. The United States fully agreed with the decision.

The refusal to hold the general elections actually gave the signal for increased terrorism by the Vietcong in the south, and the beginning of the infiltration from the north. A year later the civil war was on. This relationship of cause and effect must not be interpreted, as so often happens, as the provocation by non-compliance with the armistice of the righteous wrath of Ho Chi Minh. Politics are more realistic: When Ho Chi Minh realized that the conquest of the south, which, in spite of his military victory over the French, had been snatched away from him by the combined efforts of France, China, India, the Soviet Union and Britain, could not easily be achieved by elections, he decided to conquer the south by force of arms.

By 1960 the United States Military Aid and Advisory group (MAAG), which had taken the place of the French military advisers and their supporting forces—which by now were fully engaged in the war in Algeria—did not amount to more than a thousand. In the course of 1961, it became evident that the Diem regime was fast losing the civil war. President Kennedy, after a number of fact-finding missions had been dispatched to Vietnam and after a careful assessment of the situation, made his decision in December 1961. The number of advisers was to be increased to 16,000, and they went under the euphemistic title of "combat advisers." The mission was expanded into one designed not only to train, but also to support the South Vietnamese army, including engagement in the battle.

The fateful decision was part of the confrontation between the Soviet Union and the United States which dominated the year 1961-the Vienna meeting, the Berlin ultimatum, the building of the wall, the gigantic nuclear tests of the Soviet Union. As Arthur Schlesinger points out, "the President unquestionably felt that an American retreat in Asia might upset the whole world balance."[5]

On November 1st, 1963, a group of Vietnamese Generals mounted a palace revolt against the tyrannical regime of Ngo Dinh Diem and his brother Nhu. The intervening power, the United States, did not discourage it. The two Vietnamese leaders were assassinated and a succession of unstable governments was the result.

---

[5] Arthur M. Schlesinger Jr., *A Thousand Days* (London, 1965), 477.

The Vietcong insurgency in South Vietnam was by now massively supported by the North Vietnamese army. Under the new administration of President Lyndon B. Johnson, the discussion now turned to the question of how the war could be ended and how the intervention from the north could be stopped. The decision was finally to try graduated deterrence. On August 4, 1964, in the Gulf of Tonkin, two American destroyers, *Turner Joy* and *Maddox,* reported that they had been attacked by motor torpedo boats. This was the moment for "limited and adequate retaliation," as President Johnson termed it. It consisted in bombing the bases of the torpedo boats and of the fuel dump supplying the craft on the North Vietnamese coast. According to the modern theories of limited war, the bombing was to serve as a signal to North Vietnam, showing the United States' determination. The hope was, that Hanoi would, in view of such determination, try to negotiate and to extricate itself from the war. This hope was not fulfilled.

In February 1965, a second limited step followed, the systematic bombing of selected targets in North Vietnam connected with the war effort in the south. Yet, Ho Chi Minh could not be moved to negotiate. He actually had no reason to do so, since the regime in Saigon seemed near to total collapse and since in the United States and the rest of the western world public opinion had been mobilized against the American intervention in such a way that North Vietnam was greatly encouraged to continue the war to the end.

The different reasons for this failure are weighed by Robert E. Osgood in a full discussion of the strategic aspects of the operation. One is that the strategy of controlled escalation was basically designed to apply to confrontations with the Soviet Union. The second is that, for psychological reasons, the military nature of the targets in North Vietnam was stressed and thereby the bargaining function blurred. The third may be the deficiency of aerial bombing as a punitive device, especially when applied to an underdeveloped country. Hanoi simply did not play the game.[6]

---

[6] Robert E. Osgood, "The Reappraisal of Limited War," *Problems of Modern Strategy,* Adelphi Paper No. 54 (London, 1969), 50.

As an emergency measure, in Summer 1965, within four months 100,000 American soldiers were dispatched to South Vietnam. Their number was gradually increased and reached at the end of 1967 the figure of 485,000. With the increasing commitment, criticism mounted in the United States. It mounted to such a point that, on March 31, 1968, President Johnson had to announce his decision to severely reduce and limit the bombings in North Vietnam, and not to seek re-election in November of the same year.

A conclusion to be drawn from this extraordinary and unfortunate war is that an engagement at the side of a weak government which is seriously threatened is likely to lead to intervention of an unwanted size. It shows how easily events get out of hand, how much of the planning is done for the planners by outside forces, and how often the intervening power must do exactly what she most wanted to avoid. The plan was to help a weak government to consolidate itself, and thereby to avoid instability in South East Asia, disorder, and the danger of a major conflict. A war in Asia was, after the Korea experience, the last thing the United States wanted to engage in. The method employed for avoiding it proved ineffective.

Whatever the bitter consequences of this intervention may be, the balance of power in Asia was not allowed to tip in favor of China or the Soviet Union, or both. The question remains open whether the immense cost of life, human suffering, money, prestige and domestic harmony was proportionate to this result.

The Brezhniev Doctrine

With the intervention in Hungary in 1956 the Soviet Union had given proof of her determination not to loosen any element of the protective belt of satellite states which she had militarily occupied and consolidated as a conquest by subversion at the end of World War II. Ten years after the Hungarian events, when one or the other of the satellite countries gave signs of being attracted by the overtures of the western nations, by their economic prosperity and the freedom of their way of life, inevitably they were looking for trouble.

In the appeals for a new and freer conception of the communist system, which the Czechoslovak writer's association had made public in the summer of 1967, the chain of events began which was to lead to one of the most dramatic interventions of our time. In late fall, student's demonstrations in Prague were handled brutally by the police. Discontent among the Slovak nation with the neglect and suppression by the Stalinist regime grew. On January 4, 1968, the plenum of the Central Committee of the Communist Party of Czechoslovakia forced the President of the Republic, Antonin Novotny, to resign from the office of Secretary of the Communist Party, which he held simultaneously. Alexander Dubcek was elected in his place, the first Slovak to occupy this central post. On March 22, Novotny was forced to resign as President of the Republic and expelled from the Central Committee. In a clever move to guard against Soviet intervention, a figure respected in Moscow, General Ludvig Svoboda, a highly decorated military commander in the Red Army in the war against Germany, was elected to be head of state.

On April 5 an action program was adopted in Prague by the Central Committee, which envisaged a freer economy, freedom of choice of employment, freedom of speech, press freedom, freedom from arbitrary arrest, rehabilitation of the victims of the terroristic prosecution of the Stalinist era. The Soviet Union answered in its press with sharp criticism of the reformer's ideas. Within the framework of the Warsaw pact, military staff maneuvers were scheduled for June 20. Lest Prague not understand the signals, a number of Soviet tanks were sent to participate in the maneuvers.

The next step was to invite Prague's leading men for a discussion in Russia. Mindful of the tragic fate of Johannes Hus (the Bohemian reformer and advocate of the independence of his people, who had been cited before the council of Constance, who went under safeconduct of the Emperor, and who was convicted of heresy and burned in 1415), the Czechoslovak leaders refused to attend the meeting. In addition, they demanded the withdrawal of the Soviet forces.

With the effects of the first signals spent, the Kremlin now engaged in negotiation. At the end of June, the Soviet leaders met with the Czechoslovak leaders in Cierna na Tisou, in Slovakia near the Soviet border. The agreements reached were confirmed in a second conference held in Bratislava, in which the other members of the Warsaw pact took part. In exchange for a few secondary concessions by Prague, the Soviets seemed reconciled with the reforms in Czechoslovakia. Yet, back in the Kremlin, an "agonizing reappraisal" of the situation must have taken place. At dawn, on August 21, 1968, strategic points of Czechoslovakia were occupied by Russian airborne troops; Soviet, Hungarian, Bulgarian and Polish forces and German troops from the DDR penetrated the country. The intervenors tried, on the very day of the invasion, to set up a puppet government, similar to the Kadar government used in 1956 in Budapest as an instrument for subduing the victim. The attempt failed, since no known politician dared to accept a post in such a government. No military resistance was offered, but passive resistance and a show of extraordinary ingenuity in protecting threatened people from the Russian police, in upholding communications and in keeping the people informed of what was going on made life for the intervening power and its helpers miserable. In the space of one year, however, the spirit and the possibilities of resistance were gradually eroded and suppressed and the Soviet Union established its complete hold over the satellite, bringing it again into line with Soviet policy.

An interesting feature of the intervention is that it was clad in the trappings of a collective action of the Warsaw Pact nations. For a power of the size of the Soviet Union to overwhelm a small country like Czechoslovakia evidently no help in a physical sense by allies was required. Moscow, however, took great pains to conduct the operation not in isolation but assisted by forces of four other members of the pact. In so doing, it tried to give the intervention an international aspect and some semblance of legality.

The final consecration of the action taken against Czechoslovakia was sought by a statement of general policy. It appeared in the party newspaper *Pravda* in Moscow on September 26, 1968 in an article over the signature of Sergei Kovalyov. The leading phrases are:

The sovereignty of each socialist country cannot be opposed to the interests of the socialist world, and the interests of the world revolutionary movement.

* * * *

The socialist states respect the democratic standards of international law. They have proved this more than once in practice, by coming out resolutely against the attempts of imperialism to violate the sovereignty and independence of nations. It is from these same positions that they reject the leftist, adventurist conception of "exporting revolution", of "bringing happiness" to other peoples. However, from a Marxist point of view, the standards of law, including the standards governing the mutual relations of the socialist countries, cannot be interpreted narrowly, formally, or in isolation from the general context of class struggle in the modern world. The socialist countries resolutely come out against the exporting and importing of counter-revolution.

Each Communist party is free to apply the basic principles of Marxism-Leninism and of socialism in its country, but it cannot depart from these principles (always provided, naturally, that it remains a Communist party).

Concretely, this means, first of all, that in its activity, each Communist party cannot fail to take into account such a decisive fact of our time as the struggle between two opposing social systems— capitalism and socialism.

* * * *

It has got to be emphasized that when a socialist country seeks to adopt a "non-affiliated" stand it, in actual fact, retains its national independence, precisely thanks to the might of the socialist community, and above all the Soviet Union as its central force, which also includes the might of its armed forces. The weakening of any of the links in the world socialist system directly affects all the socialist countries, which cannot look indifferently upon this.

* * * *

. . ."self-determination" . . . would have encroached . . . upon the vital interests of the peoples of these countries and would be in fundamental conflict with the rights of these people to socialist self-determination. Discharging their internationalist duty to the fraternal peoples of Czechoslovakia and defending their own socialist gains, the USSR and the other socialist states had to act decisively, and they did act, against the anti-socialist forces in Czechoslovakia.[7]

The justification of intervention, the formulation of a legal duty to intervene by the Soviet Union as a central force, includ-

---

[7] Sergei Kovalyov, "Sovereignty and International Duties," *Pravda,* September 26, 1968, transl. *Survival,* Vol. X, No. II, November 1968 (London, 1968), 375 f.

ing armed intervention, the limitation of sovereignty and self-determination of the socialist nations by the higher interests of the other socialist peoples and, especially, the Soviet Union, contained in these pronouncements, have been termed the Brezhniev Doctrine in the West. In Moscow it was violently denied that such a doctrine did exist at all. However, the doctrine was confirmed on other occasions. Leonid Brezhniev, the Secretary of the Communist Party of the USSR, speaking in Warsaw on Juy 21, 1969 at the celebration of the 25th anniversary of the communist regime in Poland, said:

> The strengthening of the positions of world socialism as a whole, the achievements of each socialist country, are undissolvably tied in with the solidary actions of the socialist states, with their mutual help. Socialist internationalism is equivalent with high responsibility for the fate of socialism, not only in their own country, but in the whole world.[8]

In an article in the issue of August 1969 of the Czechoslovak review *Problems of Peace and Socialism* Brezhniev offered the intervention of the Soviet Union in favor of all peoples "who are exposed to aggression, who fight against imperialism, for their national, political and economic liberation, for social progress."[9] On April 3, 1970 in a speech in Budapest, he once more confirmed his doctrine.

As we have seen, the intervention in Czechoslovakia has ushered in a new concept of limited sovereignty of individual nations, and has therefore thrown open the door for great power intervention by the Soviet Union. The doctrine is similar to the concept of the responsibility of the United States toward its wards in Latin America in the nineteenth and early twentieth centuries. Adversely, the doctrine, in the second paragraph of the text reproduced above, also limits intervention. While Moscow rejects for itself the export of revolution and both the export and import of counter-revolution, it also opposes equally the interventionist tendencies of governments such as those of China or Cuba, as well as any attempt by a non-communist nation to intervene against a communist regime or movement

---

[8] *Neue Zürcher Zeitung,* July 24, 1969, Nr. 447 (Zürich, 1969).

[9] *Neue Zürcher Zeitung,* August 6, 1969, Nr. 475 (Zürich, 1969).

within another country. The rejection of export of revolution, however, is qualified; the law of the permanent class struggle may, as in the case of Czechoslovakia, and probably also in the cases of the so-called "wars of national liberation," warrant intervention by the Soviet Union.

The Nixon Doctrine

The disappointment with the intervention in Vietnam, the political crisis it had created within the United States, and the deterioration of relations with other nations which had resulted from the Vietnam war, introduced a revision of the foreign policy principles as announced by Presidents Truman, Eisenhower, Kennedy and Johnson. In the course of a tour of Asian countries, which President Richard M. Nixon undertook between July 25 and August 1, 1969, the new look was stated and explained in presidential speeches and informal remarks.

In a press conference on the island of Guam on July 25, 1969, the President said among other things:

> If the U.S.A. just continued on the road of responding to requests for assistance, of assuming the primary responsibility for defending these countries when they had international or external problems, they were never going to take care of themselves.[10]

In an exchange of formal greetings in Bangkok, on July 28, President Nixon explained that the nations of Asia can and must increasingly shoulder the responsibility for achieving peace and progress. He went on:

> The challenge to our wisdom is to support the Asian countries' efforts to defend and develop themselves, without attempting to take from them the responsibilities which should be theirs. For if domination by the aggressor can destroy the freedom of a nation, too much dependence on a protector can eventually erode its dignity.[11]

Gradually the general lines of a foreign policy doctrine emerged, which was to be applied not only to Asia, where it was originally announced, but to all parts of the world where the United States had assumed responsibilities. Its central idea is to

---

[10] *Keesing's Contemporary Archives*, (London, 1969), 23509.

[11] *The Department of State Bulletin*, Vol. LXI, No. 1574, August 25, 1969, (Washington, D.C., 1969) 154.

limit intervention. Whereas the United States would keep its treaty commitments for the maintenance of international security, it would in the future refrain from intervening in the case of internal disturbances. Assistance in such situations would be limited to material help, if requested, excluding the kind of support which would involve the commitment of manpower. This new attitude became soon to be called the doctrine of Guam or the Nixon doctrine.

The State of the Union Message which President Nixon delivered on January 22, 1970 before the Congress, summed the new policy up in the following terms:

> Today the great industrial nations of Europe, as well as Japan, have regained their economic strength, and the nations of Latin America —and many of the nations that acquired their freedom from colonialism after World War II in Asia and Africa—have a new sense of pride and dignity, and a determination to assume the responsibility for their own defense.
>
> This is the basis of the doctrine I announced at Guam.
>
> Neither the defense nor the development of other nations can be exclusively or primarily an American undertaking. The nations of each part of the world should assume the primary responsibility for their own well-being; and they themselves should determine the terms of that well-being.
>
> We shall be faithful to our treaty commitment, but we shall reduce our involvement and our presence in other nation's affairs.[12]

This represents a complete departure from the involvement with other nation's security, domestic and external, which the Truman, Eisenhower, Kennedy and Johnson administrations had so unhesitatingly accepted. It is also a departure from the Nineteenth century concept that the nearer foreign nations came to follow the American model, the happier they would be. In the future, even in American eyes, the nations of the world will themselves be responsible for their well-being, and they themselves will have to know best what the terms of their own well-being are.

Whether this concept ushers in an era where intervention becomes more and more unlikely, is, of course, not dependent

---

[12] *International Herald Tribune,* No. 27067, January 23, 1970 (Paris, 1970).

on a policy decision of the administration in Washington only, but rather on the feasibility of a policy of restraint and aloofness in the modern international environment. And it depends on how long the Soviet Union will adhere to its preposterous Breszniev doctrine in the face of a growing anti-interventionist movement.

Chapter IX

The Law Of Intervention

Legitimate or Illegitimate?

We have described intervention as an action limited in time, in which a superior power or an international organization transcends the framework of the existing relations and attempts to impose its will on a nation or lends to it its superior power, in the name of some concept of a political, legal or moral order. As shown in the preceding chapters, such actions are frequent in history and an important feature in the pattern of present-day international relations. International law as the system of law whose primary mission it is to regulate the relations of one state with another, has, quite naturally, assumed its function also in relation to intervention. A whole body of rules and concepts of public international law is concerned with intervention, and legal rights of intervention as well as prohibitions of intervention have been developed.

The efforts of providing intervention with legality when it did occur, by the powers which considered themselves entitled to intervene in other countries in the name of morality and law, are one source of the law of intervention. The defensive efforts of the smaller nations likely to become the targets of intervention are the other source of law.

An impressive list of such acts was drawn up by juridical science, together with the corresponding terms of art: interference, intercession (giving assistance to a government without being invited), intervention (when assistance had been requested), interposition (justified, when a state takes action to induce another state to respect certain rights under international law), self-help (a stronger form of interposition), co-operation (use of

155

force in redress for an illegal act for the benefit of another), reprisals (harmful act designed to punish a wrong-doer), retortion (lawful act in reply to a harmful yet legal act), humanitarian intervention (justified when directed against excessive injustice), supervision (the US over the whole of Latin America), regional control (the US over Central America).

The effort was addressed to the question of the distinction between legal and illegal intervention. An elaborate terminology of course does not advance a better understanding of the distinction between legal and illegal acts. All the cases examined are interventions according to the definition offered by political science. The proposed distinctions, in actual fact, are much less distinctions of a legal nature than descriptions of different methods and different strategies of intervention. Whether legal or illegal can only be judged on the merits of the case, on the motivations of the governments involved and their relationship to the existing international law, as embodied in treaty obligations or universal rules. Legality is not dependent on the method employed and the label attached to the act by the actors. What these earlier discussions offer is not much more than the abortive attempt to press political acts into a conceptual system.

In this context the argument was advanced that certain international conflicts because of a specific legal quality cannot be submitted to arbitration or judicial settlement and, therefore, entitle a state to procede unilaterally and possibly to intervene by force in another state. This argument, derived from Emmerich von Vattel's writing (1758), has been rejected by modern theory.[1] Contemporary juridical science assumes that there is no conflict in international law inherently unsuited for submission to peaceful settlement. It admits, however, that states, of course, may attempt change and adjustment for purely political reasons and with arguments of an entirely political nature, without even alleging that an injustice under international law is to be redressed.

In the early years of this century, the expanding economic and financial involvement of Europe and North America in the developing world—such a world existed *avant la lettre*—made

---

[1] Paul Guggenheim, *Lehrbuch des Völkerrechts* (Basel, 1951), 604.

intervention for the recovery of debts a frequent feature. It was resented by the underdeveloped debtor nations and recognized by the great powers, involved in colonial competition as they were, as a possible source of conflict between one another. Therefore, the Second International Peace Conference at The Hague had, in 1907, addressed itself to this specific question. The result was the *Convention respecting the limitation of the employment of force for the recovery of contract debts* of October 18, 1907. It became known by the names of its chief architects, the former Foreign Minister of Argentina, Luis M. Drago, and the former American Ambassador Horace Porter, and has been called the Drago-Porter Convention.

The only materially relevant article of the convention, its Article 1, provides that:

> The contracting powers agree not to have recourse to armed force for the recovery of contract debts claimed from the government of one country by the government of another country as being due to its nationals.
> This undertaking is, however, not applicable when the debtor state refuses or neglects to reply to an offer of arbitration, or, after accepting the offer, prevents any *compromis* from being agreed on, or, after the arbitration, fails to submit to the award.[2]

This text made armed intervention illegal in a typical case where it was frequently applied. Intervention, however, becomes legal, when the defaulting debtor does not comply with the legal proceedings provided for by the treaty. Collecting debts for one's nationals being an extremely weak motivation for a government to use armed force against another nation, the Drago-Porter Convention is proof that for more serious offenses intervention was, at that time, universally considered as legal.

Legal title for intervention was also derived from natural law and the laws of geopolitics. Elihu Root, the Secretary of War of the United States, expressed in a speech delivered in Chicago, on February 22, 1904, an impressive formulation of such thoughts when he spoke in justification of President Theodore Roosevelt's armed intervention in Colombia in preparation for the building of the Panama Canal. He said:

---

[2] James Brown Scott, *The Hague Peace Conferences of 1899 and 1907* (Baltimore, 1909), Vol. II, 357.

> By the rules of right and justice universally recognized among men
> and which are the law of nations, the sovereignty of Colombia over
> the Isthmus of Panama was qualified and limited by the right of
> other civilized nations of the earth to have the canal constructed
> across the Isthmus and to have it maintained for the free and
> unobstructed passage.[3]

The law of limited sovereignty would re-emerge, 64 years
later, not as a consequence of geopolitics, but as a consequence
of the teachings of Marxist-Leninism.

The efforts devoted to the establishment of collective security
in our contemporary world have developed a legal system of intervention which does not start from a static view distinguishing
what is lawful or illegal under established formal rules, but rather
starts from the operational concept to ask how international
wrong can be prevented or, when committed, redressed.

Along with the universal law of intervention and the international system of intervention, rights to intervene have been
created by specific bilateral or multilateral agreements. The
classic example is the Platt Amendment of 1903.

When the United States wrested Cuba from Spain in the
war which was concluded by the Treaty of Paris of December
22, 1898, it set up a Constitutional Assembly in the occupied
country to prepare for independence. In an amendment to the
army appropriations bill, which was introduced by Senator H.
Platt from Connecticut, and which was accepted by the Congress
and signed by President William McKinley on March 2, 1903,
Cuba was required to introduce in its new constitution among
other provisions designed to implement the Monroe Doctrine,
a special undertaking to the effect that:

> the Government of Cuba consents that the United States may exercise
> the right to intervene for the protection of Cuban independence, the
> maintenance of a government adequate for the protection of life,
> property, and individual liberty, and for discharging the obligations
> with respect to Cuba imposed by the treaty of Paris on the United
> States, now to be assumed and undertaken by the government of
> Cuba.

A corresponding provision was embodied in the treaty of
May 1903 which spelled out the relations of the new state of

---

[3] "The Ethics of the Panama Question," *Senate Document 471, 63rd Congress,
2nd Session* (Wahington, D.C., 1904), 39.

Cuba with the United States. The treaty provided the basis for the interventions of 1906 and 1917. By 1933, when the Convention on Rights and Duties of States was signed at Montevideo, the treaty had become dead letter, except for the agreement on the naval base of Guantanamo; it was replaced, on May 29, 1934, by a new treaty, reflecting the good neighbour policy inaugurated by the administration of President Franklin D. Roosevelt.[4]

In the complex of agreements arrived at in Zurich and London, in 1959, setting up an independent state in Cyprus, extensive rights of intervention, including armed intervention, were conceded to Great Britain, Turkey and Greece, collectively and individually. Article 3 of the treaty of February 23, 1959, signed in London between Great Britain, Greece and Turkey states that:

> In the event of any breach of the provisions of the Treaty, Greece, the United Kingdom and Turkey undertake to consult together with a view to making representations or taking the necessary steps to insure observance of these provisions.

> In so far as concerted actions may prove impossible, each of the three guaranteeing Powers reserves the right to take action with the sole aim to re-establish the state of affairs established by the Treaty.[5]

The opposite, an agreement on nonintervention, was reached in connection with the civil war which broke out in Spain in 1936. In this instance the French government proposed principles and rules of nonintervention in the civil war, which then were individually accepted by all the European governments except Switzerland, which remarked that its neutrality was permanent and not limited to the case under discussion. The subsequent development of the policy of nonintervention and the corresponding international agreements have been dealt with earlier.[6]

One of the most frequently invoked arguments for establishing a legal right to intervene is, of course, an invitation, a request by the target society of the act. We have seen, when defining intervention, that the existence of an agreement between the in-

---

[4] David F. Healy, *The United States in Cuba 1898-1902* (Madison, Wisconsin, 1963), 150; Robert F. Smith, *The United States and Cuba, Business and Diplomacy, 1917-1960* (New York, 1960), 156.

[5] *U.S. Government White Paper of July 7, 1960* (London, 1960).

[6] 106.

tervenor and the intervened, which of necessity exists when intervention is invited, conceptually precludes the act from being called interventionary. An opposition of wills is an essential feature of the concept, and such opposition of will has to be assumed, when intervention occurs, regardless of whether a formal invitation to intervene has been issued or not. We must deal with the problem, however, for two reasons. One is, as we have seen, the existence of such agreements in the shape of treaties of intervention. They do not preclude intervention, even when existing between the intervening power and the victim of intervention, when the agreement was arrived at not with a specific, existing or imminent situation in view, but with the wide scope to create a general legal right, abrogating the rules of and respect for the sovereignty of individual nations and nonintervention. Another instance, where such agreements do not conceptually exclude intervention, is when they are concluded between nations other than the one to be intervened against, as for example in the treaties on Cyprus.

The other reason is the uncertain character of requests to intervene. In practice, many cases where intervention has been requested will be considered as intervention in the conceptual and legal sense and treated as such. Numerous examples are to be found in this book, the interventions in Lebanon and Jordan, in South Vietnam, in Kuwait, in the Congo and in Gabon. The reason is that such requests and invitations generally are doubtful. In many instances it will be difficult or impossible to ascertain whether the invitation has been made or not. It may be doubtful whether the invitation has been extorted from the victim as a first step in the course of the intervention. And in the frequently observed situation when a constituted government is fighting a rebellion, or when in a civil war two parties claim to be the legally constituted government, it may be extremely doubtful which party is entitled to speak in the name of the nation and to invite foreign intervention. For legal purposes it will, therefore, be advisable, in all cases where there is doubt, to ignore the invitation and to deal with the problem of intervention as if such invitation or request never had been issued.

The Inter-American System

Up to the end of World War II and before the former colonial empires had been transformd into a world of sovereign nations, Latin America corresponded more or less to what today are termed the developing nations. It was, as we have seen, the preferred theater of interventionism. It is, therefore, not surprising that these nations, the elites of which included a high proportion of well-trained jurists, should address themselves with great intensity to the problem of intervention. The Pan-American Union, the origin of which dates back as far as the conference of American states in Washington in 1889-1890, and which was founded in 1910, became the pioneer, not only for all the existing international institutional systems, but more specifically for the modern law of intervention.

When the Sixth Pan-American Conference opened, on January 16, 1928 at Havana, all American nations were present for the first time, and the President of the United States of America, Calvin Coolidge, attended in person. The high aim of this conference was the codification of international law for the Americas. This was not achieved, but not less than eighty conventions and resolutions were approved. One of the most controversial and most burning questions in this attempt at codification was, as one would expect, intervention.[7]

In a planned declaration on the rights of nations an *Article 3* was inserted which prohibited intervention in the domestic affairs of another nation. This declaration due to the opposition of the United States, however, was not adopted. Its delegation insisted that the right to exercise interposition should be reserved, in case violence and anarchy broke out in a member state which made action for the protection of life and property of foreigners mandatory.

The further history of the Pan-American conferences is at the same time the history of conflicting views on the right of intervention. In 1933 the United States, under the administration of President Franklin D. Roosevelt, finally accepted, at the conference of Montevideo in the Convention on Rights and

---

[7] Carlo Cereti, *Panamericanismo e diritto internazionale* (Milan, 1939).

Duties of States of December 26, 1933, the general principle of nonintervention, but with a reservation concerning Cuba. In 1936, the United States approved a general condemnation of intervention for the first time without reservations.

At that particular time the Western Hemisphere felt threatened by the growing infiltration of Fascism and National Socialism. The Monroe Doctrine of 1823 was therefore reviewed, and consultations in case of a threat to the peace of the hemisphere were envisaged. In the conferences of Havana, 1940, and Mexico City, 1945, the problem of collective security was considered with greater urgency due to the world conflict. It found final form in the *Inter-American Treaty of Reciprocal Assistance,* signed at Petropolis in 1947 and called the Rio Treaty.

The moment the principle of collective security was recognized, it became evident that, in certain cases this might also imply intervention in another state. This recognition was embodied the following year in the fundamental document of the Organization of American States.

On May 2, 1948, at Bogota, the ninth conference of the Pan-American Union adopted, the *Charter of the Organization of American States,* which came into force on December 13, 1951. In its articles 6, 15, 17, and 19 it superseded the earlier law of intervention and actually wrote the *magna charta* of non-intervention.

First of all, the Charter does away with the earlier concept of the paramount nation, which is responsible for other, smaller nations, protects them, educates them—in short, considers them as its wards, and derives from this relationship a legal right to intervene in their affairs. Article 6 provides that states are juridically equal, enjoy equal rights and have equal duties. "The rights of a State depend not upon its power to ensure the exercise thereof, but upon the mere fact of its existence as a person under international law." Therefore, even the weak nation, which is perhaps prevented by domestic instability from exercising its powers cannot become the victim of an intervention.

The central disposition is contained in Article 15, which establishes the unconditional prohibition of intervention. It reads:

No State or group of States has the right to intervene, directly or indirectly, for any reason whatsoever, in the internal or external affairs of any other State.

The foregoing principle prohibits not only armed force but also any other form of interference or attempted threat against the personality of the State or against its political, economic and cultural elements.

Article 17 adds that the territory of a state is inviolate; it may not be, even temporarily, the object of military occupation or of other measures of force, directly or indirectly, on any grounds whatsoever.

Such rigid rules are apt to come into conflict with the principle of collective security, also incorporated into the Charter, in its Articles 24 and 25. In case of an armed attack against an American nation or an aggression which does not take the form of an armed attack, the members of the OAS undertake, under the terms of the Rio treaty, to assist the victim of the aggression in the exercise of their right of individual or collective self-defense to meet the attack. This may, of course, imply the occupation of the territory of other nations and the deployment of forces, even without the consent of another nation, within the area of its sovereignty. In order to exclude such conflicts of rights and duties, Article 19 rules that measures adopted for the maintenance of peace and security in accordance with existing treaties are not considered as constituting a violation of the principle of nonintervention.

Such possibilities of conflict became especially visible when Secretary of State John Foster Dulles brought his obsession with the universal danger of communism to the American councils. At the tenth Inter-American conference which met in 1954 at Caracas, a resolution was adopted to the effect that the domination of the political institutions of an American state by the "international communist movement" would endanger the peace of America. In such an event a meeting of consultation of ministers of foreign affairs would be called to consider the appropriate action in accordance with existing treaties, especially the Rio treaty.

It now became evident that a decision of resisting collectively such communist domination might lead to collective intervention by the American states themselves in one of the states of the hemisphere. Therefore, an additional provision was introduced in the resolution, stating that these declarations of intent were designed to protect and not to impair the inalienable right of every American state freely to choose its own form of government and economic system, and to live its own social and cultural life. With this limitation, it is difficult to see how from the resolution concerning communism in an American state a legal title could flow which would justify intervention, and it was, therefore, practically nullified. If an American state chooses an economic system related to communism and the corresponding government structure, it is difficult to see how the OAS could react without violating the existing treaty provisions and resolutions.

The united front of Latin American states against intervention existed as long as the only possibility of such action was one by the United States. The front was split when more democratic regimes existing in some Republics sharply contrasted with dictatorships such as Rafael Trujillo's in the Dominican Republic, Dr. Duvalliers in Haiti, General Alfredo Stroessner's in Paraguay. It was rightly assumed that the United States, especially in the Eisenhower years, favored these dictatorships, since they seemed to be firmly anti-communist. Some Latin American regimes in turn began to play with the idea of intervention in the shape of collective action of OAS against dictators. At the consultative meeting of Foreign Ministers of the OAS at Santiago (Chile) in 1959, the idea was brought forward that the principle of nonintervention should not apply when the objective was the overthrow of a dictatorship. Now, the U.S. Secretary of State Christian Herter paradoxically became the advocate of the strict application of the principle of nonintervention. He insisted that the principle of nonintervention should always prevail and not be weakened in any attempt to impose from without a government on a nation.

The strong opposition of the majority of the OAS members against the dictators in their midst finally found expression, not in a new brief for intervention, but in a strongly worded declaration of August 18, 1959 to the effect that the existence of antidemocratic regimes violates the principles of the OAS and endangers the solidarity and the peace of the western hemisphere. In addition, a study of methods and procedures for preventing activities from abroad against established governments was commissioned.

The conclusion to be drawn from these discussions is that as soon as the strict principle of nonintervention is questioned—the reasons may be very respectable from a political or moral standpoint—the result is conflict and instability.

The League of Nations System

The central idea of the global system founded in the Covenant of the League of Nations of June 28, 1919, was collective security. The principle was laid down in Article 11 of the Covenant, according to which any war or threat of war was a concern of the whole League, and the League would take "any action that may be deemed wise and effectual to safeguard the peace of nations." The second leading idea was the undertaking solemnly entered into by the members of the league "to respect and preserve as against external aggression the territorial integrity and existing political independence of all members of the League" (Article 10).

This article implicitly contains the principle of nonintervention. Whether the League would enforce this provision safeguarding territorial integrity and political independence in the case of an intervention was dependent, of course, on the decision on the merits of the case, whether a particular intervention should be termed an aggression. It was to be expected that any victim of intervention by a great power would, in the future, invoke Article 10 of the Covenant against the interventor, and thereby oblige the Council of the League to "advise upon the means by which this obligation shall be fulfilled."

This article ran into strong opposition, for this very reason, even while it was drafted. The opposition in the Senate of the United States against the League of Nations and the Treaty of Versailles setting it up used these precepts as one of its main arguments. Article 10, in fact, was difficult to reconcile with the Monroe doctrine and with the doctrine to which the United

States still adhered that it was the warden of the Latin American nations. The government of Canada went as far as to propose in 1920 the elimination of the article from the text of the Covenant.

How far this disposition would really affect intervention was never entirely clear. A Commission of Jurists, entrusted in 1921 with an interpretation of the article, practically excluded its application in cases of intervention. The ruling was that the article concerned lasting changes in the territorial status and the political independence of a state. From this one had to conclude that interventions, which by definition are of a transitory nature, were not covered by the precept.[8]

The general tendency, in the early years of the League of Nations, was to reduce the effectiveness of the article as much as possible. This found expression in a remark by the former Italian foreign minister Vittorio Scialoja made at the fourth Assembly of the League in 1924. He insisted that the obligations of the article were not and should not be accompanied by any judicial sanction, because its aim was only to proclaim a lofty principle which in turn would, gradually, become part of the conscience of the peoples, and therefore much more effective than any compulsory provision.[9]

Based on provisions in the Treaty of Versailles, in 1919 and 1920 treaties were concluded with Czechoslovakia and Poland for the protection of the inhabitants of the corresponding state "who differ from the majority of the population in race, language or religion"—Germans, Russians and Hungarians. Under these agreements the members of the Council of the League of Nations were entitled, provided that the Council consented, to take all measures which seemed effective for the safeguard of the rights of such minorities. In effect, these treaties therewith conveyed wide authority to intervene in domestic matters of other nations.

In the peace treaty signed with Bulgaria at Neuilly on November 27, 1919, precepts concerning the protection of minorities were inserted. They mostly concerned the 70,000 Greeks in

---

[8] *Publications de la Société des Nations VII*, questions politiques 1938, 1-2.

[9] *Publications de la Société des Nations*, Ass. 1923, première commission, 17.

Southern Bulgaria. The treaty conceded a wide right of intervention by the following provision:

> Bulgaria agrees that any Member of the Council of the League of Nations shall have the right to bring to the attention of the Council any infraction, or any danger of infraction, of any of these obligations, and that the Council shall thereupon take such action and give such directions as it may deem proper and effective in the circumstances.

A similar minority treaty was concluded on August 10, 1920, with Greece, for the protection of the 150,000 people of Slavic origin, mostly Bulgarian speaking, subject to Greek rule in Thrace and Macedonia. These treaties established a right of intervention. It was never actually invoked, except in a very limited way when the League of Nations resettled a great number of Bulgarian refugees from Thrace and Macedonia.

The right of the League of Nations to take "action that may be deemed wise and effectual to safeguard the peace of nations," in its sweeping form, certainly also contained the inherent right of intervention. The Council could recommend to governments what military, naval or air force the members should contribute to armed forces to be used for the protection of the Covenant of the League. The League of Nations, however, which lacked universality and was very much centered on Europe, never had the occasion or the power to conduct an intervention in style, nor to react by force against illegal intervention. When confronted in 1931 and 1937 with the massive aggressions of Japan in China, which were claimed to be interventions, the League proved powerless and had to resign itself to inactivity.

In two instances, however, police forces were organized for the protection of plebiscites to be held under the auspices of the League of Nations: one was designed to guarantee the 1920 plebiscite in Vilna, which finally was not held. The second case was the plebiscite in the Saar. By resolutions of December 1934 an international military force, made up of detachments of four nations, was put at the disposal of the Governing Commission of the Saar by the Council and it proved effective.

In 1933 and 1934 a number of Colombian troops were earmarked as international forces of the League of Nations to assist a commission of the League which administered for a short time the area of Leticia, situated at the juncture of Brazil, Colombia and Peru, an area which was claimed by these latter two nations.

The System of the United Nations

When the foundations for the United Nations were laid at Dumbarton Oaks and San Francisco, the failure of the League of Nations to prevent the events which led to World War II and the catastrophe itself were foremost in the minds of the jurists and statesmen engaged in that great enterprise. The founders tried to eliminate all the weaknesses, as they saw them, which had undermined the first world security organization.

The result was the introduction of Chapter VII into the Charter of the United Nations of June 26, 1945. According to its Article 39, the Security Council of the United Nations shall determine the existence of a threat to the peace, breach of the peace, or act of aggression and shall make recommendations or take measures to maintain or restore international peace and security.

The measures it may take have a wide range, from interruption of economic relations to action by military force. Instead of the formulae of collective security as contained in the Covenant of the League, which were hoped to be self-enforcing, the center of the stage is now occupied by the Security Council and its wide powers, which are politically very effectively limited by the rule of unanimity of the five permanent members of the Council.

The paramount power of the world organization is, however, also subject to juridical limitations. In Article 51 the right of self-defense, individual or collective, in case of an armed attack, is expressly reserved. And in a most prominent position, in Article 2 of the Charter, a prohibition for the United Nations to intervene in domestic matters of the members is stated:

> 7. Nothing contained in the present Charter shall authorize the United Nations to intervene in matters which are essentially within the domestic jurisdiction of any state or shall require the Members to submit such matters to settlement under the present Charter;

but this principle shall not prejudice the application of enforcement measures under Chapter VII.

We have, therefore, in the United Nations system an absolute prohibition, addressed to the world organization itself, to intervene in domestic matters of members states. Intervention, however, is not clearly defined. The prohibition includes direct action by the coercive powers given to the organization, and it includes direct intervention which would consist of forcing submission of domestic disputes within a nation to a settlement under the Charter, in analogy to international disputes.

This prohibition addresses itself to the very organization as such. No corresponding disposition exists which is addressed to individual members or to regional organizations which the members may join. Two paragraphs of Article 2, however, when they prohibit threat or use of force in international relation, can be construed as an implicit prohibition of intervention. They state:

> 3. All Members shall settle their international disputes by peaceful means in such a manner that international peace and security, and justice are not endangered.

> 4. All Members shall refrain in their international relations from the threat or use of force against the territorial integrity or political independence of any state, or in any manner inconsistent with the purposes of the United Nations.

These very general principles did not prevent, as we have seen, the American intervention in Greece in 1947, the Soviet intervention in Czechoslovakia in 1948, and the Soviet sponsored North Korean intervention-aggression in South Korea in 1950. This latter moved the United Nations to clarify its concept of intervention and to strengthen *expressis verbis* the condemnation of intervention which is inherent in the Charter.

The Fifth General Assembly of the United Nations adopted on November 17, 1950 the resolution *Peace through Deeds,* which was introduced by eight nations: Bolivia, France, India, Lebanon, Mexico, Netherlands, United Kingdom, and the United States. The essential passage reads as follows:

> *Condemning* the intervention of a State in the internal affairs of another State for the purpose of changing its legally established government by the threat or use of force,

1. *Solemnly* reaffirms that, whatever the weapons used, every aggression, whether committed openly, or by fomenting civil strife in the interest of a foreign Power, or otherwise, is the greatest of all crimes against peace and security throughout the world;[10]

Accordingly, an absolute prohibition in very strong terms exists against individual intervention, insofar as it assumes forms which can be called aggression, open or by subversion.

The United Nations' responsibility for peace-keeping is supported by the central position of the Security Council and its right, under Chapter VII of the Charter, to determine the existence of a threat to the peace, breach of the peace or act of aggression, and to take measures accordingly. Such measures may be simple recommendations and appeals to the parties concerned. As soon as they go further, they become interventions in the true sense of the word. They may consist of coercive measures summed up under the term "sanctions," such as partial or complete interruption of economic relations, the severance of rail, sea, air, postal, telegraphic, radio and other means of communication, or the severance of diplomatic relations. If these sanctions appear to be inadequate or have proved to be inadequate, the Security Council may take military sanctions, including demonstrations, blockade or operations by air, sea, or land forces of members of the United Nations. In practice, such interventions have taken the form of military action in only two cases: in Korea in 1950 to 1953, and in the Congo-Katanga from 1961 to 1962. In all other instances the intervention consisted of sending observer teams or security forces, the mission of which was not to fight but to separate antagonists and, by informing the Security Council of infringements of the orders given to the opponents, to deter further infringements and aggressions.

United Nations peace forces and observer teams—important instruments for the performance of interventions in conflicts— are surprisingly enough, not mentioned in the Charter. The basic document rules only that the members make available to the Security Council armed forces, assistance and facilities, including rights of passage. It is generally admitted, however, that the United Nations possess the legal competence to establish and

---

[10] Gen. Ass. Res. A/380 (V).

operate military forces, without specific authority for it in the Charter. This is an inherent capacity of the organization, based upon the programmatic Article 1 of the Charter. As the International Court of Justice stated in 1949 in an Advisory Opinion:

> Under international law, the Organization must be deemed to have those powers which, though not expressly provided in the Charter, are conferred upon it by necessary implication as being essential to the performance of its duties.[11]

The United Nations has made, as we have seen in the preceding chapter, wide use of this right to intervene by military force in order to prevent international conflict or to separate the combatants and to supervise eventual truce arrangements when conflict has broken out.

The right and capacity, however, is limited to international conflicts, to situations and acts which endanger international peace and security. Intervention in domestic conflict is excluded by Article 2(7), which prohibits the settlement of domestic matters under the provisions of the Charter. In order to intervene in situations of this kind when the Security Council or the General Assembly deem it necessary, a threat to international peace and security must exist or be construed. To link unwelcome forms of government with peace in general, and to pretend that such governments are a danger to peace, is an old and universal practice. We have only to remember President Truman's speech of March 12, 1947, in which he said "totalitarian regimes imposed on free peoples. . .undermine the foundation of international peace."

This system was applied in relation to Spain. Several members of the United Nations strongly advocated some kind of international intervention with the object of overthrowing the dictatorial regime headed by General Francisco Franco and to establish a democratic regime. In order to enable the United Nations to take such action, which by Article 2(7) is prohibited not only with respect to members but to "any state," Poland requested the Security Council in April 1946 to declare the existence of the Franco regime a threat to international peace

---

[11] For a full discussion of the question of the inherent rights: Finn Seyersted, *United Nations Forces in the Law of Peace and War* (Leyden, 1966), 151 ff.

and security. To examine this delicate question, the decision of which was apt to set an important precedent, the Council set up a sub-committee of five members; on June 6, 1946, the sub-committee submitted a majority report, with a minority dissenting. The opinion was that the activities of the Spanish government did not constitute an existing threat, but rather a potential menace to international peace. The committee suggested that these findings be transmitted to the General Assembly with the recommendation to sever diplomatic relations with Madrid. A corresponding decision of the Security Council was prevented by the veto of the Soviet Union, which insisted that the Franco regime was not only a potential but an existing threat and that the Council and not the Assembly should decide on sanctions.

Accordingly on December 12, 1946, the First Assembly of the United Nations recommended that members recall their diplomatic representatives from Madrid. It invited the Security Council to consider measures for bringing about a democratic regime in Spain. Most members complied with the recommendation. This constituted intervention in a very mild form, and it proved ineffective. On November 4, 1950, the Fifth General Assembly revoked its recommendation.

In order to bring a situation which was exclusively of a domestic nature under the jurisdiction of the United Nations and to open the door for intervention, the Security Council passed a resolution on April 1st, 1960. It dealt with the incidents which had occurred in Sharpville, in the Republic of South Africa, in March, 1960. The resolution stated:

> The situation in the Union was one that had led to international friction and if continued might endanger international peace and security.[12]

On November 17, 1966, the General Assembly adopted a resolution calling upon the government of the United Kingdom to intervene against the regime headed by Ian Smith in Rhodesia. It stated that this government was illegal since it was a racist minority regime. The resolution demanded that Great Britain take the necessary measures, including in particular the use of force, to put an end to that regime. In a subsequent resolution

---

[12] Security Council Res., *UN Documents*, S/4300 (1960).

of December 16, 1966, the Security Council stated that the situation in Southern Rhodesia constituted a threat to international peace and security.[13] It confirmed the appeals to apply economic sanctions made in earlier resolutions, including an embargo on imports and exports. It was the first time economic sanctions under Chapter VII of the Charter were voted, and it was undoubtedly an intervention, since its object was a change of the political structure of the target society.

We see, consequently, that within the United Nations a legal doctrine has developed which permits intervention against governments or forms of government which do not correspond to the views and ideals professed by a majority of the members of the organization. The basis of its application is invariably the invocation of a threat to the peace and to international security, which permits circumvention of the nonintervention clause of Article 2(7). The doctrine appears somewhat artificial. When in relationship to such regimes—unfriendly governments—a threat to the peace develops, it is generally not originated by the regime which is the object of the planned intervention, but the threat to international peace originates rather from the opposition of others against that regime.

The whole system of nonintervention resulting from the text of the Charter of the United Nations has been waived, in one particular instance, by its Article 107. It states that nothing in the Charter shall preclude action against a state which during World War II has been an enemy of one of the signatories of the Charter, taken as a result of that war. Article 53 adds a provision to the effect that such actions may be taken without the authorization of the Security Council.

Since 1968 this provision has been alluded to several times in Soviet political oratory, always within the framework of the general campaign of intimidation and slander conducted against the Federal Republic of Germany. Yet, Articles 107 and 53 of the United Nations Charter have undoubtedly become obsolete with the passage of time since the war. France, Great Britain and the United States relinquished these rights towards Germany in the agreements concluded in Bonn on May 26, 1952 and in

---

[13] Gen. Ass. Res 2151 (XXI); Security Council Res. 232 (1966).

Paris on October 23, 1954. All nations which were "enemies" in 1945 but one—Germany—have become members of the United Nations: Austria, Bulgaria, Finland, Hungary, Italy, Japan, Rumania. They are, therefore, signatories to the Charter, and it could be argued that they now, in turn, may take recourse to Article 107. This would be an absurdity and is proof that the Article has lost its meaning. Actually nobody would seriously ever claim that an unlimited, discretionary right to intervene in these states existed under Articles 107 and 53 of the Charter. These precepts have to be considered as of a transitory character, designed for the early period after the war, and do not alter in the least the system of intervention now prevailing; this system excludes individual action and reserves collective action to cases where a threat to international peace and security can be invoked.

The preoccupation with interventions remains one of the permanent features of the United Nations. Similarly, it is one of the main problems of the Organization of American States and of the Organization of African Unity. In the fall of 1965, when the Twentieth General Assembly convened in New York, the intervention by the United States in Vietnam was at its height; and the landing of the Marines in Santo Domingo, in which the OAS had saved the United States from an embarrasing unilateral involvement, the Cyprus conflict, in which Turkey had threatened intervention and the subversive activities directed by Ghana against its neighbors were fresh in everybody's mind. On December 21, 1965, the Assembly, therefore, unanimously issued a declaration concerning intervention, evidently designed to be another charter of nonintervention. It does not introduce any new legal provisions but is rather a restatement of a well known and accepted doctrine, but in this instance clad in the verbiage of United Nations documents.

In its preamble, the declaration reaffirms the charters of the Organization of American States as confirmed at the conferences of Montevideo, Buenos Aires, Chapultepec and Bogota, the charters of the Arab League and the Organization of African Unity. Equally, it confirms the decisions of the conference of African and Asian states held at Bandung, those of the first conference of heads of state or government of non-aligned countries held at Belgrade in 1961, the program for peace and international cooperation adopted at the end of the second conference of heads of state or heads of government of non-aligned countries held at Cairo, and the declaration on the problem of subversion adopted at Accra by the African heads of state and government.[14] The essential passages of the resolution of December 1965 contain the following statements:

> Every state has the inalienable right to choose its political, economic, social and cultural system, free of any interference by any other state. No state has the right to intervene, directly or indirectly, for any reason whatever, in the internal or external affairs of any other state. Consequently, armed intervention and all other forms of interference or attempted threats against the personality of the state or against its political, economic and cultural elements are condemned. All states must refrain from organizing, helping, instigating, financing, encouraging or abetting armed activities of a terroristic or subversive nature designed to violently change the system of government of another state or to intervene in the internal struggles of another state. Nothing contained in the declaration shall be interpreted as affecting in any way the application of the dispositions of the Charter of the United Nations for the maintenance of international peace and security, especially those in Chapters VI, VII and VIII.

The essence of this statement adopted by more than one hundred governments is the condemnation of individual intervention in all its aspects and forms. The express reservation of the application of the dispositions of the Charter of the United Nations for the maintenance of international peace and security replaces all intervention by single powers by the collective action of the world organization.

Article 52 of the Charter authorizing regional arrangements or agencies to deal with matters relating to the maintenance of international peace and security as are appropriate for regional action gives collective action by such organizations and agencies equal status with those of the United Nations themselves. Among organizations authorized to intervene regionally, in conformity with their own rules, only such entities are recognized under Article 52 are those whose form and activities are consistent with the purposes and principles of the United Nations. Among this group may be counted bodies such as the Organization of Ameri-

---

[14] Gen. Ass. Res. 2131 (XX).

can States (OAS), the Arab League, the Organization of African Unity (OUA) founded in 1963 in Addis Ababa, the *Organization Communauté Africaine et Malgache* (OCAM), formed in 1965 out of the *Union Africaine et Malgache*. These are entitled to wear the mantle of the United Nations, whether they use their potentialities for collective intervention or whether they prefer to have recourse to the universal organization.

We would exclude from this category, of course, all regional alliances such as the North Atlantic Treaty Organization (1949), the Warsaw Pact (1955), or minor arrangements like CENTO, SEATO, ANZUS and the many African arrangements such as OERS, UDEAC, UEAC, or European organization like EEC, EFTA. Their purpose is limited and they themselves do not aspire to be the equivalent of a regional organization in the sense of the Charter of the United Nations.

Parallel with the generally stated right of collective intervention by the world organization in case of a threat to international security and peace, rights of intervention have been created by particular conventions. The Convention on Prevention and Punishment of the Crime of Genocide of December 9, 1948, which has drawn much inspiration from the Agreement on the Prosecution and Punishment of the Major War Criminals of the European Axis of August 8, 1945, contains the corresponding provision in its Article 8. Under the terms of this article the signatories of the treaty may call upon the competent organs of the United Nations to take such action under the charter as they consider appropriate for the prevention and suppression of acts of genocide. Persons committing genocide, conspiring to commit genocide or publicly inciting such crime, whether private individuals, public officials or constitutionally responsible rulers, shall be punished according to the laws of the signatories of the convention. The signatories undertake to enact the corresponding legislation. An example of such legislation is the Penal Code of the Federal Republic of Germany, in its version of August 25, 1953, Paragraph 220 a. (Genocide). This article threatens with imprisonment for life any person who tries to destroy a social group distinguished by its nationality, race, religion or national allegiance.

Since it is unlikely that an official or a head of state or government can be brought before any court of law of any nation for such an offense by any power within his own state, the implementation of all these dispositions can hardly be imagined otherwise than within the framework of an intervention by force of the United Nations or authorized by it.

A wide field of collective intervention may emerge as soon as universally binding treaties on arms control have been adopted. Such treaties will deal of necessity with inspection and safeguards, all of which have aspects relating to intervention.

Article III of the Treaty on the Non-Proliferation of Nuclear Weapons of July 1, 1968, obliges the non-nuclear-weapon states party to the treaty to accept safeguards in accordance with the International Atomic Energy Agency's (IAEA) safeguard system. This presupposes, within the provisions of the treaty and the agreements concluded with the IAEA, activities of international inspection teams on the territory of the contracting parties. The inspectors will report on non-compliance with the treaty obligations, whereupon the IAEA may apply sanctions. Its own sanctions are very mild indeed. They include information of other parties to the treaty, termination of assistance given and recovery of the materials made available to the defaulting nation by the IAEA.

None of these—inspection and sanctions—are, of course, interventions in any narrow sense of that word. Yet, a report of the inspectors which discloses a consistent non-observance of the IAEA's safeguards and of the treaty obligations may, in view of the relevance of the acquisition of nuclear weapons for international peace and security set in motion the machinery for the restoration of international peace and security by the United Nations under Chapter VII; in turn, this may lead to intervention, including intervention by armed force.

It is interesting to note that governments are fully aware of these inherent possibilities of intervention included in agreements on arms control. One of the main arguments of the Federal Republic of Germany against signing the Nonproliferation Treaty was precisely that it may open the door to claims for intervention in domestic affairs of the Republic, even without any infringement being committed, by the mere fact of the involvement of a nation in inspection procedures.

Collective v. Individual Intervention

We have seen that up to the end of World War I general agreement seemed to exist that within the boundaries of international public law intervention by individual powers could be exercised. A power would, when certain conditions were fulfilled, take the law in its own hands. With the rise and decline of the League of Nations, with the activity of the Permanent Court of International Justice, and with the strengthening of the Inter-American system, the period between the two wars can be described as a period of transition. The right of the great powers to intervene became more and more doubtful and suspect.

With the emergence of the United Nations, the International Court of Justice, and the regional organizations, the period after World War II ushered in the new look. It is largely based on two new features:

One. The equality of nations is fully recognized in international law. The hegemony of the two world powers exists as a political fact, yet is not recognized as a valid or permanent concept in law. A rule of international law which cannot be applied to the strong as well as to the weak, to the small as well as to the large, is no longer considered to be good international law. The influence of small nations as a factor of political life has grown. This is partly due to the balance of power existing between the super-powers; to a certain degree this neutralizes their influence and forces them to seek accommodation with much smaller nations. But it is also due partly to the role which small nations and their spokesmen are allowed to play in the councils of the United Nations.

Two. The instruments for the protection of the interests of nations in their international relationships have been greatly modified, expanded and improved. Nations are expected to avail themselves of the possibilities offered, especially by the United Nations, to achieve their specific goals. Under this protective screen sovereignty has become almost absolute—absolute, however, only in its passive sense that nobody may interfere in the domestic matters of a state. In its active meaning, which gives the state untrammeled freedom of action, sovereignty has been severely limited by the system of collective security.

The result is that intervention by an individual state is universally considered as illegal and prohibited. Since in the international environment adjustment and enforcement remain necessary to a certain degree, the solution lies in collective action. Only collective intervention, within the framework of an international organization recognized as representing a collective force for the maintenance of peace and security, and under its rules, is understood as legal.

Even a treaty arrangement freely entered into, in which a nation waives all its rights to nonintervention and in advance accepts individual intervention by another signatory as a legal act, cannot stand up to the modern legal concept of intervention. Only when such a treaty is equivalent to an alliance, a treaty of mutual assistance and is a permanent basis for cooperation, then, of course, it makes law. Yet, in that case, no intervention is conceivable in the mutual relationship since no conflict of wills exists. An intervention clause for the case of a conflict within the alliance could, when applied, be opposed by invoking the general law of nonintervention.

By contrast to classical international law, the prohibition of intervention by force of arms is stated in contemporary juridical science as a principle without exception. In modern literature and practice only intervention on behalf of the United Nations or assimilated organizations seems to be admitted as lawful.[15]

Whatever form intervention may take, whatever label be attached to it by the interested power—self-help, humanitarian intervention, development aid, self-defense, intervention under a treaty authorizing it, assuming responsibility for a ward, supervision, limited sovereignty—all these acts are not admitted under contemporary international public law. Wherever the situation seems to warrant action interfering with the domestic affairs of a state, it must be taken by a duly authorized community of nations.

---

[15] Krzystof J. Skubiszewski, "Use of Force by States," *Manual of Public International Law, ed.* Max Sørensen (London, 1968), 758.

This is the position of modern international law. It is clear enough. On the other hand, political science, political writing, especially when it originates in either of the world powers, sometimes tries to revert to Nineteenth century concepts. It rejects the principle of nonintervention with the simple argument that "Powerful nations do not, and cannot, adhere to it."[16]

16 Andrew M. Scott, "Nonintervention and Conditional Intervention," *Journal of International Affairs,* Vol. XXII, No. 2 (New York, 1968), 209.

Chapter X

The Strategy Of Confrontation And Intervention

The Tools of Confrontation

The strategy of confrontation and the strategy of intervention have one essential feature in common: They are strategies of limited use of force, applied with the view to attain a national goal, but excluding the danger of escalation of the conflict into a wider conflict.

The strategies differ basically in their relation to the power structure of the contestants: Confrontation may occur between a great power and a small nation, if this latter is willing and able to oppose its will to a larger power, or between equals or near equals. Intervention is only thinkable in the relationship between a powerful nation and a much smaller or at least much weaker nation. If the two opponents are equals or near equals, there will be confrontation, open conflict, armed clash, war, limited or general, but not intervention.

The instruments of confrontation occupy, as we have seen in examining recent confrontations in their historical setting, a wide range, the whole range, in fact, of the strategic potentialities of a nation. This does not imply that from this wide array of weapons one or the other may be selected to conduct a confrontation, as the golf player selects his club. On the contrary, the typical, characteristic feature of confrontation is, that all available instruments suited to the occasion have to be brought into play simultaneously, similar to the lawyer who uses all his arguments, including facts, their interpretation and points of law, if he wants to win his case.

No confrontation may be waged without appealing to the nonmilitary forces at the disposal of a nation, as exemplified by the confrontation over the Suez Canal, where the outcome was unfavorable for France and Great Britain because they had neglected sufficient diplomatic preparation and the accompaniment by psychological warfare.

Confrontation is in our time generally thought of as being necessarily nuclear, since the most spectacular confrontations have been waged between the two super powers. As we have seen in preceding chapters, this assumption is not sound. There have been confrontations which were, in spite of the existing nuclear capabilities of one or both contestants, clearly of a conventional type; the Berlin blockade, the Cuban missile crisis, and the *Pueblo* incident are examples. There have been confrontations between nations which were or are not in the possession of any nuclear arms, such as China and India, Indonesia and Malaysia, Turkey and Greece.

Confrontation with the threat of conventional force is perhaps less fraught with danger, in an absolute sense, than when nuclear threats are involved. However, for the nations immediately concerned, the danger can be relatively so great that it may approach the nuclear threat in its effect for the outcome of the confrontation. Modern military technology and modern military skills have had a far-reaching and significant effect. Conventional war becomes so destructive that it appears less and less as a rational method of solving bilateral problems. Technology and new methods provide such intensity to conventional war, that it soon becomes an intolerable strain. The effect is that nations very different in size, population and economic importance become very similar to each other when they ask themselves what damage they can inflict on the other and what damage they must expect in return.

In conventional confrontation—which is, as we have seen, always a mixture of threats of military force, diplomatic and psychological means, and other elements of strategy—the military front line continues to play an essential role. What one opponent thinks he can do to the other, and what the other thinks can be done to him, and vice versa, will greatly influence the outcome. In conventional confrontation with a larger power or a great power, with the increased mobility and fire power of modern armies, when it comes to a show-down, even a smaller nation may expect to wage successfully a defensive war, at least during a limited space of time. Therefore, in a strictly strategic meaning, we have among the nonnuclear weapons states many more pairs of equals than in earlier times. This automatically increases the possibilities of confrontation, while it minimizes the possibilities of intervention in the strict acceptance of the concept which we propose.

Modern conventional weapons systems have become the "equalizer," much more than the atomic bomb which some analysts, not very convincingly, have tried to construe as such. They are wrong when they refer to the relationship between a world power and a medium or small nation, since those who hold such opinions assume that even a world power would never accept any kind of damage which could be inflicted on it by the nominal nuclear force of a small opponent. This is not likely to be true, since in a confrontation between a world power and a medium or small nuclear power the greater opponent has to face only limited damage and is certain to survive with an overwhelming proportion of its population, its economy and infrastructure, whereas the smaller one faces total and inescapable annihilation.

The short war between India and Pakistan in September 1965 and the six-day war between Israel and the Arab countries of June 1967 supply ample evidence of this development. Hence the reluctance to engage in conventional war and the effectiveness of conventional threats in confrontation, even between pairs of unequal powers. In this context, we must check with history whether we are not wrong. Alfred Nobel, in 1880, believed that his invention of dynamite would make governments so reluctant to expose their forces to destruction by the new explosives that war would become impossible. At the beginning of the Twentieth century the opinion prevailed that modern weapons—the machine gun, field artillery, the heavily armored ship—would make war necessarily a very short war. This proved conspicuously wrong, and we do not want to repeat this error. Yet the development of air power, mechanized weapons, stronger conventional explosives, and transmission and observation systems has been so spectacular, that it dwarfs earlier technological breakthroughs. Objectively also the nature of conventional war is changed. It assumes not only other dimensions but other qualities.

It is not the quantity of the forces marshalled against an opponent in a confrontatioon, but rather their quality, which counts. Among quality one of the most impressive, visible elements is diversity. Quantity is difficult to ascertain in the modern world. In the Nineteenth century it was relatively easy to know the number of soldiers of two opposing armies and the number of cannons of two opposing navies. In the first half of the Twentieth century one easily ascertained the number of divisions which confronted each other. Because the relative weight and effectiveness of armaments were approximately known, their number was an indicator of strength relationship.

Today we may know the number of divisions, airplanes, missiles of different categories, and warships, and the number and location of fortifications and bases. But in spite of all this numerical information, we are unable to ascertain exact quantities, because we do not know the effectiveness of each item, and, therefore, are in doubt whether or not to include it in our calculations. What is the caliber of each nuclear warhead? How many warheads are carried by each missile? How accurate is the delivery system? How solidly are the missiles "hardened," and how well protected are other elements of the opponent's forces? How effective is the opponent's civil defense system? How effective is his war economy?

We judge, therefore, rather by qualitative differences, including diversity of strategic potentialities. We ask: Has he nuclear weapons or not? Has he an intercontinental delivery system? Has he strategic mobility? Is he organized to wage psychological and subversive war? Has he a space program? Is he well-connected with the United Nations or with a regional system of security? Is he a member of an alliance, and of which? What is his reputation in bargaining?

In confrontation, therefore, the display of diversity of sophisticated strategic systems and instruments, including those of diplomacy, is more likely to decide over the outcome than the number of items listed in the Military Balance.[1]

The Use of the Tools in Confrontation

Confrontation is a form of tacit negotiation, similar to limited war, perhaps a form of limited war. What Thomas C. Schelling brilliantly describes as the conditions by which decision is brought about in limited war, applies fully to confrontation and the elements which determine the outcome:

(1) tacit agreements or agreements arrived at through partial or haphazard negotiation require terms that are qualitatively distinguishable from the alternatives and cannot simply be a matter of degree;

(2) when agreement must be reached with incomplete communication, the participants must be ready to allow the situation itself to exercise substantial constraint over the outcome;

*   *   *   *

In sum, the problem of limiting warfare involves not a continuous range of possibilities from most favorable to least favorable for either side; it is a lumpy, discrete world that is better able to recognize qualitative than quantitive differences, that is embarrassed by the multiplicity of choices, and that forces both sides to accept some dictation from the elements themselves.[2]

In nuclear and more especially thermonuclear confrontation the most conspicuous tools are the existing warheads with their corresponding delivery systems. Their number does play a role, as evidenced in the Cuban missile crisis which developed around the problem of how the Soviet Union could increase the number of missiles able to reach the continental United States. Yet numbers are, as we have seen in practical experience, much less important than the existence of certain systems, which, for the purpose of confrontation, may be useful, even when they are only represented by prototypes. The effect of their existence depends on the possibility to impress on the mind of the opponent their novelty, their destructiveness, the resolution to use

---

[1] This refers to the annual publication of the Institute for Strategic Studies, London, *The Military Balance.*

[2] Thomas C. Schelling, *The Strategy of Conflict* (New York, 1963), 75, 77.

them, and perhaps the ability to convince him that they might be used irresponsibly.

In August 1961, two weeks after the building of the wall separating the Soviet sector of Berlin from the Western sectors, when the Soviet Union, in one of the most spectacular moves of the confrontation over Berlin, announced that nuclear tests in the atmosphere would be resumed, the procedure corresponded exactly to this pattern. Mention was made of the "unequalled cosmic flights around the earth" of the Soviet cosmonauts Gagarin and Titow. Major Gagarin's ballistic flight in space around the earth took place on April 12, 1961, and was the first feat of this kind. It was promptly seized upon by the Soviet strategists of confrontation as a powerful means of pressure because of its novelty and uniqueness. This mention was linked with the information that now thermonuclear warheads of 20, 30, 50 and 100 megatons were available. Nobody seemed to care whether there were two or three or one hundred such warheads in the Soviet arsenal; Moscow counted on the shattering effects of the advance its space program had taken over the United States,[3] and the colossal explosions which were staged in the sky of the far north.

The psychological corollary accompanying the material threat with the possibility of nuclear annihilation is as important as the weapons systems to which allusion is made. The opponent must be convinced that he is facing an adversary who is willing to take increasing risks, and that he is willing to lift the conflict to ever higher rungs on the ladder of escalation, if the opponent does not surrender. This accompaniment may include the projection of the image of a cold and calculating mind, which reluctantly, yet inexorably deploys the power at its disposal. It may also include the image of an irrational frame of mind, capable of reckless actions when provoked.

The attitudes adopted by Soviet Chairman Khrushchev in the U-2 confrontation of 1960 in Paris certainly corresponded to his general character, to his frame of mind, and to his deep irritation by domestic opponents and by his Chinese critics. Yet by displaying freely his capacity for invective and irrationality he

---

[3] 56.

wanted to impress on the American government the certainty
that the risk of nuclear war had grown to a serious possibility.
The act was repeated at the session of the General Assembly
of the United Nations in New York. Again in the display of
violence which Khrushchev presented to the international forum,
his liking for histrionics, his irrepressible temperament played a
role. Not every detail of the act was premeditated. Yet the
whole preparation of the expedition to New York, the accompanying declarations, the prevailing situation of the nuclear
confrontation lead to the conclusion that Khrushchev wanted to
be judged as a dangerous man, able to perform the most reckless, irrational acts when he did not have his way.

An important and effective instrument of psychological
warfare in the bargaining process is always the ability to impress
the fear on the opponent that things may "get out of hand."
This may be done by conveying the idea that, for reasons outside
one's own control, the conflict will escalate unless the opponent
surrenders. Such reasons given or hinted at may be indomitable
temperament, irresistible domestic pressures, pressures of an ally,
impossibility of allowing a precedent being created, and the
limited powers of a negotiator.[4]

Another essential is the presentation of the object of the
confrontation as being out of proportion to the risk being
taken. It is important to show that the stakes are really not
worth the risk. The redistribution which is sought will be
presented as a minor one, the concession demanded as a final
one, and it will be insisted that surrender at this point would
not only put an end to the confrontation but eliminate all
future conflict.[5]

That the fear of irrational behavior of the Soviet Union's
ruler was firmly anchored, by methods of psychological warfare,
in the minds of the decision makers in Washington in the early
sixties was evidenced more than once. In addition, the Soviet
negotiators successfully tried to create the impression that they
did not understand the United States' position and that they
could not bring themselves to believe that the position of firm-

---

[4] Fred Charles Iklé, *How Nations Negotiate* (New York, 1962), 83.
[5] *ibid.*, 85.

ness of the United States was serious. By this procedure they created the conviction that they were underestimating Washington's resolve. President Kennedy and his advisers were beset by the fear of "miscalculation" on the side of the Russians. One of the results was the Vienna meeting of President Kennedy with Chairman Khrushchev in June 1961, where the President rather naively tried, by patiently restating the United States' position, to dispel such danger of "miscalculation."

Whether the confrontation be nuclear or conventional, according to the military threat involved, the outcome of the bargaining process depends largely on the political environment which has been created for the occasion. The attitudes of allies, of uncommitted and neutral states, and of opponents influence in many ways the decision. The expression these attitudes find in the councils of the United Nations by far outweigh the actual decisions the world organization may or may not take. These attitudes are conditioned by public opinion as expressed by its organs of mass communication. The effect on the confronting powers is a subtle one and difficult to assess, yet it exists. Since in confrontation a tacit process of bargaining goes on, a competition in risk-taking, a contest of resolve—in short, a psychological process— the fact whether the responsible and often lonely actors of the confrontation feel that they are supported by many, or opposed by many, has a far-reaching effect.

The outcome of every confrontation, whatever the size and power of the contestants, whatever the characteristics of the tool most conspicuously employed, always depends on the skillful use of the totality of the available instruments within the given environment.

Military Intervention

Instruments of intervention are all those political and military means which confer on a nation a position of marked superiority over the nation which is the target of the operation. Without unquestionable inequality between the opponents conceptually there is no such thing as intervention. Among equals, the contest of will would take the form of confrontation, use of force, war.

For our purpose, we start by examining the strategies of intervention by force, and then go on to look at methods of intervention short of military force. The fact that instruments and methods are discussed does not, of course, imply that the use made of these instruments and methods is necessarily considered as legitimate and justified.

Up to 1914, the classical instrument of armed intervention was sea power. Gunboat diplomacy was the civilized way in which the great powers—Great Britain, France, the United States, the Netherlands, Germany, Austria, Italy, Russia—used to deal with less civilized and minor nations in Asia, Africa and Latin America. It consisted of "showing the flag" in harbors or on the rivers of an unruly country, firing shells into the waterfront of some settlement or into the jungle, putting ashore a landing party, occupying the capital city by the marines, or blockading one or several ports. The Russians, more oriented towards land operations, would move in a division and burn down farms and villages.

After World War II, the strategy of intervention became more demanding. Today, by symbolic gestures very little may be achieved. A strategy for sustained actions has developed.

The first element of the strategy of intervention is, true to the nature of the operation, to limit it. In the choice of the instrument and the methods, the possibility to end the intervention and to extricate oneself from the engagement will always have to be kept in mind. To avoid force from spreading beyond the limits of the area selected for intervention and to prevent the involvement of other powers is the politico-military problem number one. When the engagement becomes more general, the plan to conduct a limited war operation is defeated. Intervention may be swallowed up by something much greater and riskier, as was the case in South Vietnam.

To make sure that the operation remains limited, and that there is a chance for success, political and military intelligence and the apt interpretation of its results is absolutely crucial, even more than in any other situation of conflict. The lessons of the Franco-British intervention against Gamal Abdel Nasser at Suez in 1956, the invasion of Cuba at the Bay of Pigs in 1961 by

US—supported refugees, the American intervention in South Vietnam, the Soviet intervention in Czechoslovakia of 1968— all of these point unmistakably to the importance of political intelligence. In all these cases the political situation in the target society, the state of public opinion vis-a-vis the government which was to be overthrown or established, was not correctly assessed. The examples point also to the great difficulty of determining a correct interpretation of intelligence reports when a great wealth of factual information is available. Surprises will always be in store for an intervenor. So great is uncertainty in situations where a state engages in a venture such as modifying the power structures of another society, that it is not advisable to undertake the smallest operation of this kind, unless the intervening government is prepared, willing and able to risk escalation to extended, but still "limited," warfare.

The military instruments of intervention are, in the words of the Charter of the United Nations "demonstrations, blockade and other operations by air, sea, or land forces." Air power proved in World War II an important weapon, but by far not the decisive weapon as projected by its impassioned advocates such as Giulio Douhet (1869-1930), William E. Mitchell (1879-1936), Alexander Seversky (b. 1894). Yet, being conservative, most military men continued to cling to the view that air force was the appropriate means to break the will of an opponent. Hence the conclusion that it was the best instrument for intervention. When South Korea was invaded in 1950 by the army of North Korea, it became clear, from the very outset, that American air power, even when combined with overwhelming sea power, could not protect the invaded country. In 1956, on the occasion of the intervention in Egypt, the British High Command, true to the shibboleths of "victory through air power," planned to introduce an "aero-psychological phase" consisting of eight-to-ten days of bombing of the Egyptian air force and points of military and psychological interest in Egypt, yet sparing the enemy army and the population. It was hoped that this method would provoke the fall of Abdel Nasser and the collapse of Egyptian resistance, whereupon an unopposed landing would take place. The "aero-psychological operation" finally was reduced to six days. It started on October 30, 1956, and the first landing followed on November 5.[6] This air operation was, of course, completely ineffective and only served to arouse public opinion in the whole world against the adventure. In Vietnam, the use of air power was effective in the tactical and operational environment. Its strategic use in controlled escalation, designed to bring the North Vietnamese government to the negotiating table by limited bombing of carefully selected targets, approved daily by the political authorities, again came to naught.

The unlimited use of air power in World War II did not break the will of resistance of peoples and governments as the examples of Great Britain, Germany and Japan show. We even know that the two atomic bombs used against Japan did not actually bring about surrender, but only helped the Emperor and his advisers to overcome the resistance of the war party against a surrender which had become necessary and had been advocated by the most responsible Japanese circles much earlier.

Limited use of air power is obviously even much less effective. Since in intervention only limited use can be considered, the instrument is ineffectual and not adapted to the needs of such situations. The limited, selective use against symbolic targets will soon show to the population concerned that the bombing is not as devastating, as dangerous as it had been pictured. It will convey the impression to the unsophisticated mind, which does not follow the intricacies of strategic calculation, that the aggressor lacks resolve; in short that it is a "paper tiger." When aerial demonstrations are not followed by devastating blows—and they cannot be followed by such, since the operation has to remain limited—they will raise the spirit of resistance instead of breaking it.

Air power has actually acquired a new dimension, since its usefulness for logistic support and tactical lift has come to the forefront, and sometimes outweighs its importance as an instrument of actual combat. In this capacity, however, in interventionary war, air power runs into another difficulty which reduces its usefulness. It is as a rule dependent on rights to

---

[6] General Beaufre, *Die Suez-Expedition, Analyse eines verlorenen Sieges* (Berlin, 1968), 81.

overfly neutral, or uncommitted countries or countries openly hostile to the intervention. The Netherlands had great difficulty in carrying troops and supplies by air to Indonesia when it tried to fight the movement for independence in 1946 and 1947, and to New Guinea in 1962. These were not interventions, yet the cases are illustrative of the difficulty encountered by air power in world-wide operations. Airports suitable for landing supplies to intervening forces will, in most cases, be inadequate, and they can easily be immobilized.[7]

Similar considerations apply to sea power. It may have been effective in general war between sea powers, as seen by Admiral Alfred Thayer Mahan (1840-1914). It was effective in the era of gunboat diplomacy. Yet in interventionary operations in our modern time, navies will encounter the same limits to their effectiveness as air forces, insofar as their fighting capacity is concerned. It is different in the case of their capacity for logistic support; there they still are the most effective and most reliable instrument. They use the lanes of the high seas up to the target area, and no unfriendly government may interfere with their movements.

As to actual military operations in connection with intervention, sea blockade, which was such an effective means in the Nineteenth century and the first half of the Twentieth century, has probably lost much of its value. First, air transport gives full freedom of movement for persons, in spite of the naval blockade, and will overcome most of the hardships which may be caused by a blockade of limited duration. Second, blockade in peacetime, as an instrument of intervention, being illegal in international law, is bound to arouse such international criticism and opposition that it would probably be more harmful to the doer than to the defending party. The blockade or "quarantine" as an instrument of limited war in the Cuba crisis was of course an entirely different operation. It was part of a confrontation and the basis for a credible threat of escalation, and as such, effective in the general context of the then prevailing situation.

---

[7] Neville Brown, *Strategic Mobility* (London, 1963), 159.

Sea power remains a most effective instrument of intervention when used for a sustained, yet limited deployment of military forces in the target area. Organized as an amphibious force for establishing beachheads including against opposition, with appropriate landing craft and under carrier-borne air cover, sea power seems to be—militarily speaking—the most promising means of intervention in a great variety of cases which may be imagined in the present-day environment.

New technologies for landing, for unloading containers by helicopters or by barges carried on board larger ships, make amphibious operations of the future widely independent from port facilities. Fast delivery vessels and pre-positioned supply ships for such operations provide maximum flexibility and speed for interventionary operations of the amphibious type.

The Marine Corps of the United States is the best known and the most efficient and most powerful instrument ever conceived for such operations. It will be organized in the near future so as to be able to move 75% of two divisions with their attached air wing over a distance of almost 1000 Kilometers in a day, fully equipped for the building of a beachhead against strong opposition.

The British Navy maintains a much more modest, yet in its small way effective, instrument for amphibious operations; it is able to move at least one complete brigade group in one lift. Air cover is provided by aircraft carriers. Whereas the American system is definitely designed to overcome strong resistance at the beaches, the British system is rather planned for unopposed landing of a fighting force—in British parlance a "red carpet" landing, in American parlance an "administrative" landing. By its very character it reflects on the one hand the limitations imposed by the economic weakness of a country like Great Britain, on the other hand a political choice, which infers that interventions of the future will be by invitation (and therefore not interventions in a narrow sense) rather than against opposition by the intervened.

As a reply to the western power's increased capability for amphibious operations which are especially suited for intervention, the Soviet Union developed, beginning in 1966 and 1967, capabilities for intervening in far away theaters of conflict. The giant Antonov NA-22 transport plane, an equivalent of the American C-5A, was shown for the first time in 1967. At the parade on the occasion of the Fiftieth anniversary of the October Revolution, for the first time marines were presented. The navy was expanded and deployed in a way more in line with the global interests of the Soviet Union. As an article in the Yugoslav publication *Review of International Affairs* pointed out, the insistence on increased strategic mobility is designed "to counter the imperialist strategy of local and restricted wars with its own weapons, the weapons of local and restricted war."[8]

In the confrontation over the Suez Canal in 1956, over the Congo in 1960 and over Cuba in 1962, the Soviet Union ostensibly lacked the general purpose forces which would have enabled her to threaten credibly with escalation from confrontation to intervention on the spot. Moscow, therefore, had to limit herself to moves of nuclear confrontation. The Cuban incident was especially humiliating, since it demonstrated to the whole world, including communist governments, that the Soviet Union, unless it wanted to risk a nuclear exchange with the United States of America, could not come to the assistance of any distant ally. In the six days war in the Middle East in 1967 probably no intervention was ever considered as necessary, but, if planned, it would have been practically impossible for the Soviet Union.

The rather unstable character of the regimes on which the Soviet Union rests its influence in the non-European world, such as the United Arab Republic, Syria, Lybia, Iraq, Algeria, North Korea, North Vietnam, Cuba, quite naturally leads to the conclusion that at some date intervention might be necessary in order to sustain a friendly government. Hence, the Soviet decision to move towards world strategic mobility is most plausible.

The advantage of strategic mobility assured by sea power, especially when supported by carrier-based air force, rests on the fact that it is practically invulnerable to political attack before

---

[8] Andro Gabelic, "New Accent in Soviet Strategy," *Review of International Affairs,* November 20, 1967 (Balgrade, 1967), transl. *Survival,* Vol. X, No. 2, February 1968 (London, 1968), 46.

it intervenes. Forces of intervention dependent on bases in foreign countries, whether land or air forces, cannot freely be used in the present day political environment, as the British and the Americans have experienced.

Since the collapse of its colonial empire France has developed highly mobile air-transported forces specially organized for intervention in Africa. They consist of one division called *division d'intervention,* organized in parachute and marine brigades with supporting elements. Close cooperation with the *forces d'intervention interarmées* is assured, which means cooperation with the amphibious forces, the navy and the tactical air force. The mission of these forces is to support African governments bound to France by defense treaties, or to steer political developments in the general area of French-speaking Africa. These defense treaties are leftovers from the colonial era and are practically agreements between the French army and the African armies. The African component of the forces of intervention, exclusively Marines, is stationed at the western tip of Africa in Dakar, in the center at Fort Lamy and Brazzaville, and in the east at Diego Suarez on Madagascar.

These forces, as we have noticed, may be airlifted at very short notice to any point of Africa when intervention is considered a necessity. In addition to their principal role, they also maintain base facilities and the arsenals from which the African armies may draw logistic support, which, in turn, as we shall see, is an influential weapon of intervention.

The principle of nonintervention has acquired a dominant position in international public law, and most governments and world public opinion adhere to it. Therefore, despite the impressive array of weapons for military intervention in the hands of a few powers, even the most limited operation of this kind is surrounded by great political dangers for the intervenor.

In addition, the cost of the sophisticated instruments of amphibious and air-transported operations which we have just described, and the colossal expense involved when they are actually deployed, makes military intervention today a risky, and in its effects on the own economy an unpredictable affair. The Suez intervention of 1956 cost Great Britain at least L100,000,000 and precipitated a withdrawal of capital from England which within a few days would have made the devaluation of the Pound inevitable.[9] When we remember that intervention for the recovery of private debt was, in the Nineteenth and early Twentieth centuries such a frequent feature as to originate the Drago-Porter Convention of 1907 restricting it, we perceive the fundamental change. The enormous cost of modern operations, due to the extremely costly technology available and therefore applied, would in most instances dwarf, in one day, the amount of the loan expected to be recovered.

For these reasons, the instruments for clandestine intervention have been developed, not only by powers such as the Soviet Union which traditionally are accustomed to operate by subversion, but also by nations which traditionally would rather favor more orthodox procedures. This type of intervention operates by infiltration of arms and men into the target country, and then by subversion from within. The political effectiveness of this kind of interventionary warfare is based on the fact that the intervening power can try to disclaim responsibility. The effectiveness from a more military point of view is based on the fact that the forces of subversion and of subversive war are relatively immune from the effects of powerful means of defense such as sophisticated weapons systems. They are apt to mobilize in many areas parts of the population of the invaded territory against the defender. In practice, this kind of intervention will probably be successfully conducted where a movement of opposition, hostile to the government and friendly to the intervenor exists. In a thoughtful book, the French Colonel Albert Merglen has pointed out the great potentialities of this instrument of warfare.[10] We may assume, indeed, that intervention, under the pressure of the forces decidedly opposed to policies implying any meddling with domestic matters of other peoples, will more and more rely on clandestine procedures. Subversion may be, in the future, the only viable form of intervention.

---

[9] Neville Brown, *op. cit.*, 67.
[10] Albert Merglen, *La guerre de l'inattendu* (Paris, 1966).

Intervention and Nuclear Power

Military force is used in intervention as a threat, when intervention is conducted in the shape of confrontation. Since this method is frequently applied and sometimes successfully, the question immediately comes to one's mind whether the most impressive threat, the threat with nuclear force, is an effective instrument of intervention. Will not, in the future, the nuclear weapon powers simply choose this powerful means when they want to intervene in another nation's affairs?

Recent history seems to point in the opposite direction. Nuclear threats have been used in confrontations, but until now, never in intervention. Neither before nor during the intervention of the United Nations in Korea, which was an intervention by the United States, nor during the crises of the French forces in Indochina, nor when American assistance to South Vietnam became armed intervention, were atomic threats used. It is true that in 1954 at the moment of the crisis in Indochina, the use of atomic bombs to save the French forces at Dien Bien Phu was discussed in Washington. It is true that during the Vietnam War voices have been heard which advocated limited nuclear demonstrations. But all these proposals have been readily discarded as not feasible. Far from using the nuclear threat, the United States government has been at pains to reassure its own public opinion, as well as that of its allies and its opponents that the use of nuclear weapons was not considered.

As long as the strategic equilibrium between the United States and the Soviet Union exists and remains the basis for the coexistence of the super-powers, nuclear threats against third parties as a means of achieving limited objectives are out of the question. This is particularly true when in an area in which intervention is considered as a possible course of action, the interests of both world powers are involved. Since Moscow conceives its responsibility for furthering "wars for national liberation" as universal, and since Washington insists that its security depends on "public order" everywhere, the areas of non-interest have considerably shrunk. These areas are practically limited to the territory of the super-powers themselves and, on the Soviet side, the satellite belt, on the American side the NATO area, or at least the Western European sector of it. Turkey, Greece and Scandinavia certainly would not be considered by the Soviets as a zone of non-interest.

Another feature of modern strategy severely restricts the use of nuclear threats in intervention. It is the concept of deterrence. Military power is conceived today in the first place as an instrument not to be actively used but to prevent antagonistic nations from using theirs. A nuclear threat which achieves the objective of an intervention would be considered as equivalent to the deployment and use of force. Use of force, whether nuclear or conventional, is contrary to the concept of deterrence. It breaks its spell. In the conceptual framework of a strategy of deterrence or dissuasion the uncertainty as to the resolve of the antagonist and as to its actual strength and readiness is one of the operating factors. The actual employment of one's physical force, which automatically invites the use of counterforce, will dispel this uncertainty and thereby nullify the effect of deterrence. Even great powers, whose physical capability to overwhelm the nation which is the object of the intervention is beyond any doubt, are to use restraint if the instrument of deterrence is to be kept intact.

Non-military Intervention

The use of military force, is, as we see, in contradiction with the prevailing rules of public international law, highly objectionable in the eyes of an awakened public opinion and less and less likely to yield the easy results so frequently obtained in the Nineteenth and the first half of the Twentieth centuries. Therefore the question arises whether the use of the instruments of modern economic and technological interdependence is not a more promising tool of intervention.

The simple use of economic power to influence the structures or the decisions of another nation would not, at the outset, correspond to the definition of intervention. One element of it, the convention-breaking character would be missing; probably the limitation in time would also be missing. Therefore, we will not regard the normal interplay of economic power in the relationship of nations great and small, which of course may deeply influence the will of a government and hence its decisions, and even the power structures, as falling under the concept of intervention. We will only admit one special kind of economic relationship and its effects on policy as perhaps belonging to the realm of intervention—economic and technological aid.

Decolonization has created a great number of new sovereign nations, which for obvious reasons jealously guard their newly acquired independence; yet many of these are still economically weak and politically unstable. The economic weakness is derived most often from factors of geography, popular character and from the colonial background, which favors monocultures and production of raw materials rather than a diversified agricultural and industrial activity and diversified exports. Monolithic economies promote social instability and hence a lack of rational political attitudes and traditions. For these reasons, those nations depend on some kind of outside support. Such support has replaced the investment of money and talent and skills which the former colonial powers used to make in their overseas possessions, and also compensates the loss of the stable markets which they offered to their colonies. Development aid has become a necessary condition of the economic and social progress of the new nations. In many cases, as for instance Algeria, Egypt, India, imports of food on a non-commercial basis are a question of life and death for wide sectors of the population.

Dependence on aid—rather than economic aid itself—is the instrument which may be used in an interventionary way. Economic or technological help may induce a government to do what the nation bent on intervention wants it to do—such as adhere to an alliance, break an alliance with another government, sign economic agreemnts, give concessions for the exploitation of the sub-soil resources, concede rights to establish military bases. Yet inducement by gifts belongs very much to the same category of motivation as inducement by normal diplomatic persuasion and action, which is not interventionary. All these actions lack an essential of intervention: They are not directed at the power structure of the target society.

The only case we can think of where the gift of economic and technological assistance is directed at the power structures, is limited in scope and time and differs from former attitudes, and therefore may be called an intervention, is the case where such assistance is given to a government confronted in its own territory by a revolutionary movement, or when it is involved in international conflict, the outcome of which will modify the political system. Such aid would have to be considered interventionary. All the objections and criticism reserved for intervention are usually marshalled against assistance given in such situation. Only a policy of neutrality would then avoid the suspicion of intervention.

A spectacular example of such a situation was the civil war in Spain of 1936 to 1939. The two parties at war, and not only the parties immediately concerned, reacted to the slightest economic discrimination with the accusation that a third government was taking sides—and had therefore intervened—in the conflict. Another example is yielded by the civil war in Nigeria which broke out on May 30, 1967 and lasted until 1970. Anybody who came near the two contestants of the conflict, Biafra and Nigeria, in whatever mission or function one may imagine, even of a purely economic or humanitarian nature, was likely to be suspected to be an intervenor.

In these and similar situations the dividing line between intervention and nonintervention is not marked by objective criteria; the difference is made by intention. We cannot speak of intervention when the act is not designed to defend some established rule of policy, morality or law, or when its author does not intend to change the power structure of the target society.

It may be argued that dependence of a government on foreign assistance is really the situation where the giving of economic or technological aid becomes an equivalent of intervention. When a government has staked its prestige on an ambitious development plan, which in turn depends on assistance given from abroad, such a government becomes vulnerable. Assistance then grows into a condition of stability, progress or survival, at least of survival of the regime in power. When in such a situation assistance is suddenly withheld, it will cause considerable deprivation and may produce the disruptive effect on the power structures which the intervening power wants to achieve.

Experience with this weapon of intervention, however, is inconclusive. When the United States and Great Britain withdrew in 1956 their offer originally made to Egypt to build the Aswan Dam, the government of Gamal Abdel Nasser was not overthrown. And when the Soviet Union in 1960 abruptly withdrew the experts from China, the disruption caused in the plan of development did not bring about the collapse of the dictatorship of Mao Tse-tung. Weaker and unstable governments of smaller countries might be more vulnerable. But it is difficult to see why in facing a weak opponent whose overthrow is planned, an instrument as subtle and as difficult to handle as the withdrawal of assistance should be selected, when it is much easier to achieve the aim by some deployment of limited force, perhaps clandestinely.

Since economic and technological assistance is admittedly designed to bring certain values to the recipients and to move them to adapt their power structures and their way of life to the ideals and views of the donor—whether he be an advocate of socialism or of liberal democratic government—aid and assistance certainly may have the effect of intervention. The nation which lavishes gifts on a target society may so intensely wish to achieve the goal it visualizes, that it may come to believe that it actually intervenes decisively in the domestic affairs of the target nation. The recipient may be so intensely aware of the deep influences radiating from aid, that he, in turn, conceives the idea that he actually is the target of intervention. Between the bureaucracies of the donor and the aid-receiving nation, a relationship of mutual trust and interdependence may develop, which exposes them, on either side, to criticism as being a "tool of foreign interests." In spite of these impressions, these beliefs on both sides of the line, the parties concerned may be wrong, and we may not be in the presence of intervention. The results of such interferences are so unpredictable, that economic and technological aid really lacks the main characteristics of usable tools of intervention. And in most cases, the definition we have suggested for limiting the concept in order to permit a useful investigation, does not cover the great variety of activities connected with foreign aid. The conclusion, therefore, is, that economic and technological aid given to another nation should be considered separately, under its own terms of reference, and not be assimilated to intervention.

The result of the investigation is different when we consider a sideline of economic and technological assistance, military aid. Assistance given in the shape of delivery of military hardware and software, of arms and ammunitions and of training, is not military intervention, and rather a special sector of economic and technological assistance.

Military aid is, in many cases of unstable governments, the condition of survival of the regime in power. The government would be overthrown when it cannot rely on an army relatively well equipped with American or Russian or Czechoslovak or French or British firearms and trucks, and kept happy and on good terms with the governing circles, which keep the sources of such gifts flowing. Therefore, as we know, military aid is given on a large scale throughout the world.

This is not necessarily intervention. When it is a permanent feature in the relationship between the aid-giving nation and the receiver, then we may call it influence, involvement, dependence, but not intervention. To this category belongs the lasting close cooperation between the French army and a series of armies in French speaking Africa. Military aid is there supported by the installation of training facilities on the receiving side's own territory, which may be equivalent to the presence of a small foreign garrison.[11] The relationship is not interventionary in spite of the fact that, by agreement between the military men on both sides, governments may be initiated or terminated at any time.

The mutual relationship is strengthened when the military logistics of the receiving country are permanently oriented toward the sources of supply offered by the donor. That this limits independence of the receiving side is obvious. Therefore

---

11 J. M. Lee, *African Armies and Civil Order* (London, 1969), 115.

sovereign governments tend to shake off, when they can, such permanent bonds. Guinea for instance turned from France to the Soviet Union for assistance, and Mali from France to the United States.

Another method of maintaining sovereign independence in spite of dependence on foreign military aid is to split up the assistance sought between different sources. An example is given by the Congo-Kinshasa. Beginning in 1964, General Mobutu. with the sound advice received from the United Nations, divided military assistance by concluding bilateral agreements with different nations. He turned to Belgium for assistance in organizing and training the army and for training centers. He secured assistance in the training of parachutists from Israel; Canada provided assistance for the navy, Italy for the air force, and the United States supplied material for all the forces. Similarly Ethiopia has maintained its independence by chosing different sources of supply for its military needs.

That military assistance, however, may become intervention is best evidenced by the effort we have just mentioned to diversify such assistance. As in economic aid it is rather not the giving, but the withholding, which may become an interventionary step. A government of a developing country engaged in police operations against tribal unrest or against an opposition group will be extremely vulnerable to the interruption of supplies of ammunitions and vehicles. If the aid-giving government decides suddenly to interrupt the flow of assistance, then it is easily conceivable that the power structures break down. If the other conditions of the definition are fulfilled, there is no doubt that such a step is conducive to intervention.

The question has been asked whether the decision of the French government in June 1967 to withhold delivery of 50 *Mirage* aircraft already sold to Israel was an act of intervention. Intervention it was in the loose sense of the word when used to describe any political act affecting the outcome of some international conflict. Intervention in the strict sense it was not, since France did not intend in the least to bring down the government of Israel and did not aim at bringing about an ideal order of things in the Middle East; rather she tried to improve her relations to the Soviet Union, to endear herself to the Arab countries, and to antagonize the United States.

In Latin America, the armies depend to a high degree on foreign assistance, less for their training than for the supply of modern and sophisticated material. Since these forces have almost no strategic mission in the true sense of the word as guardians of the external security of the nation, but are almost exclusively an element of the domestic social and power structure, the provision of arms or the withholding of arms to Latin American armies will in most cases have a direct bearing on the government structure or the governing personnel. In spite of the fact that Latin America is even more sensitive to intervention than any other part of the world, military assistance has hardly been considered by the Latin-Americans themselves as a strategy of intervention. The reason is that the most nationalistic element of the nation, the armed forces, depend largely on arms deliveries, and if they do not object, nobody will object.

The conclusion is, therefore, that military assistance is an effective instrument of intervention only in cases where previously a relationship of dependence has been built up and where discontinuing such assistance may operate like a shock on the political structures of the target society. Yet, we may speak of intervention by such means only in those cases where we are certain that an interventionary intention existed, and that such an operation was really undertaken with a definite aim in mind.

A skeptical observer aptly remarks:

"Intervention may be distinguished from other types of influence by the simple criteria of whether the regime or the opposition groups, respectively, favor or disapprove of what is being done. What is assistance to one observer may appear as intervention to another.[12]

We have to deal, finally, with the problem whether propaganda for a political ideology is an instrument of intervention and hence part of interventionary strategies. Under the definition we have given for intervention it is conceivable, indeed, that a propaganda attack, as a pure act of psychological warfare, may

---

[12] Howard Wriggins, "Political Outcomes of Foreign Assistance: Influence, Involvement or Intervention?" *Journal of International Affairs*, Vol. XXII, No. 2, (New York, 1968), 219.

constitute an intervention. Yet, whether intervention has, or has not occurred is a question of degree.

Assuming that Cuba suddenly launches a propaganda attack against another Latin American government, appealing to the masses to rise, to the army to overthrow the constituted powers, it may be argued that it is intervention. Yet, this could reasonably be done only in cases where the government attacked is already so unstable, for domestic reasons or on account of terroristic and subversive activities conducted from the outside, that the propaganda attack is relevant. The psychological attack has to be a decisive element, apt to actually influence the outcome of a domestic conflict which developes as a consequence of such ideological propaganda.

Assuming that the Soviet Union suddenly intensifies the ideological and propagandistic attacks on the government of the Federal Republic of Germany, and in a degree which clearly is convention-breaking, we would still not assume that this is equivalent with intervention. The reason is that such an act would not be relevant. It would not be capable of decisively influencing the political development in a society as stable as the German one.

The activities of propaganda organizations as well established and active as the United States Information Service, with its libraries and centers all over the world, come as near as possible to ideological interventions. That they sometimes are considered as such is reflected by the fact that branches of such services are regularly the objects of destructive mobs when a conflict between the recipient and the United States exists. Yet this tool of political and ideological propaganda is not to be considered as an instrument of intervention. Its potentialities for basically influencing a society are too limited to be of political relevance to the outcome of a political struggle.

Similar considerations apply to the Communist Parties in the non-communist countries. They are powerful instruments of ideological propaganda. Some are more, some are less, some not at all in the service of the Soviet Union. Their activity must not be termed interventionary, since they are parts of the national political structure and as such only indirectly instruments of foreign influence. Only in cases where the direction of the party is assumed by a foreign power, the party armed from abroad and directed towards a thrust against the power structures of the target society, does the operation become intervention. This was the case during the Spanish civil war in its later periods, when control of the Republican government and of its armies had been assumed by Moscow through the intermediary of the Communist Party; or again in 1948 in Czechoslovakia when the social-democratic government was felled. But in such extreme cases, the party activities have already far outgrown the domain of ideological warfare.

In conclusion, the whole field of non-military intervention presents a great variety of puzzling problems. They can be solved by applying strictly the definition of intervention given above, and by asking the question whether its five essentials are present. This is more than an exercise in semantics. Since nonintervention has grown in the course of the 1960's into a rule of international public law and into a political principle which commands widest respect in public opinion, it is important to decide whether or not we are confronted in a conflict, with strategies of intervention.

It may be argued in summation, that most non-military interventions are not interventions at all.

Chapter XI

Confrontation, Intervention And The Peoples

Accepted Form of Conflict Solution

In the politico-military environment of the last third of the Twentieth century the need and the desire to limit conflict has become a central preoccupation. This does not imply that the possibility of conflict and the likelihood of conflicts between states and within nations is diminished. On the contrary. Never have there been in history so many independently organized actors, and there have never been so many points of contact between them. The fronts on which clashes of interest may occur have multiplied.

Maximized possibility of conflict is not offset by maximized forces of order and stability. The group of antagonistic great powers, which in spite of their antagonisms were linked by some bond of solidarity, by their common *sacro egoismo,* and which undertook to police the world, has foundered in the sea of blood and tears of two world wars. The world security organization which replaced the hegemonial group of the great powers is constantly operating, but from a position of weakness. This is characteristic of its methods yet does not altogether exclude successful intervention. Instead of one hegemonial force, which was visualized when the United Nations was founded and provided with its Security Council, two world powers emerged, the two entirely different in outlook and in their relationship to other nations. Not their concerted will, but the uncertain equilibrium between their antagonistic policies has become the paramount force which finally polices the world.

Paramount, yet weak. So weak and uncertain is this force, that the sovereign nation has enormously gained in stature. This is due to an element of domestic development: The increase of the centralized power of the state, which in the historical process started at the end of the Eighteenth century has reduced the number and the role of the intermediaries between the individual and the state. That increase nears completion in our time, and it is one of the strongly formative elements of the new nations of the developing world. The strengthening of central power in individual nations is necessarily reflected in their international behavior: They protect jealously their sovereign might. The international organizations, which have grown so much in number and outwardly enjoy such a dominant position, have become, above all, instruments for the protection of the sovereignty of their individual members.

Conflict is bound to exist in such a world, especially since the settlements after the last war and the decolonization have left so many incongruous situations with built-in instabilities. The technological environment that we have created for ourselves, however, has made conflict so destructive and so dangerous, that it is in the highest interest of all those immediately concerned, and of humanity as a whole, that the settling of conflicts by war-like acts be avoided and, when they occur, limited locally and in the amount of violence applied.

Thus confrontation, as a method of waging conflict without approaching the threshold of destructive extremes, occupies a most prominent place in international relations. Confrontation has become an accepted form of antagonistic international intercourse. Without the worldwide audience of more than a hundred nations it would fail to be what it is. Confrontation settles problems only insofar as public opinion attributes victory to one side, defeat to the other. And actually, the peoples of the world seem to have accepted with some kind of gusto the role thus assigned to them, to be the arbiters of worldwide confrontations.

Confrontation will be with us as long as there are sovereign nations with conflicting interests. Everything leads us to believe that this will be a long time. What one can hope is, that by universal restraint in the show and use of force—whether as a result of the fear of escalation to universally devastating war or of higher political insight or moral maturity—confrontation will remain a test of will and skill, good luck and might, an instrument to adjust what must be adjusted by means short of war.

A Blunt Weapon

Intervention, the other form of antagonistic intercourse in an environment which tries to limit the extent and the intensity of conflict, has undergone a profound change, which is similarly conditioned by the change in hegemonial structures.

As an instrument of policy, intervention is diametrically opposed to the concept of absolute sovereignty. This opposition finds its political expression in the formidable array of governments and complexes of public opinion against intervention when it threatens or occurs. It has found expression in public international law; the principle of nonintervention has been promoted to the rank of a paramount rule.

This development, however, does not go unchallenged. The challengers are the super-powers, which, according to certain views "do not, and cannot adhere to it."[1] Intervention is for them an essential instrument for the protection of their interests and their security. Since they look at their security as at a worldwide problem, they cannot be indifferent towards any development which changes the *status quo,* even in geographically remote areas, even in outer space.

The conceptual conflict between nonintervention and world power interests which thus has developed finds its solution in the universal acceptance, by the super-powers and the small nations alike, of the principle of collective security and, derived from it, the principle of collective intervention.

The principle of collective intervention, defensive and offensive, finds expression in the Soviet pronouncements which we have come to call the Brezhnev doctrine:

> The achievements of each socialist country, are indissolubly tied in with the solidary actions of the socialist states, with their mutual help.[2]

---

[1] Andrew M. Scott, "Nonintervention and Conditional Intervention," *Journal of International Affairs,* Vol. XXII, No. 2 (New York, 1968), 109.

[2] Speech at Warsaw, July 21, 1969.

President Johnson put the *credo* of mutual intervention, both defensive and offensive, when he spoke of Latin America in the following terms:

> We will join with the other OAS nations in opposing a communist takeover in this hemisphere.
>
> We will join with other OAS nations in pressing for change among those who would maintain a feudal system.[3]

The General Assembly of the United Nations confirmed the principle of collective intervention by maintaining the right of the world organization to act in defense of collective security, in these terms:

> Nothing contained in the declaration (of nonintervention) shall be interpreted as affecting in any way the application of the dispositions of the Charter . . . for the maintenance of international peace and security.[4]

All of these are assertions that multilateral and international intervention may be conducted legally within the framework of some statutory proceedings for promoting or defending "socialist achievements" or peaceful "change of a feudal system," or for "the maintenance of peace and security." All of this is supposed to be for the good of the peoples. But what is the attitude of the peoples of our modern world towards all these good intentions to promote their happiness?

What we find is that intervention of any kind, individual or collective, whatever its intention, is resented and in most cases not accepted. Even when invited and requested by governmental authority it will be considered objectionable by a sector of the target society. And when we study the power structures of the modern state, it becomes more and more unlikely that intervention may be conducted successfully. Intervention may only be undertaken, as we have seen, by a large unit, by an individual state or an international organization, against a much smaller unit. This is part of the definition. Strategically, intervention in order to be effective, has had to be conducted, in the past as in the present, like a surgical operation, swiftly, silently,

---

[3] Speech at Baylor University, May 28, 1965.
[4] Declaration of December 21, 1965.

and practically without giving the organism time to realize what happens and to react. In the modern world the conditions where this may be done seem to have disappeared.

The Rules of the Game Have Changed

The rules of the game changed. In the past a conflict was resolved, an intervention was successful, when the capital city of the target society or another geographical seat of power was occupied by the intervenor. The government then would frequently become the obedient servant of the occupier, or else be replaced by another government which would fulfill his wishes. The collapse of France in 1940—in spite of being, of course, not the result of an intervention but of a great international war—illustrates the transition. The constituted government under Marshal Petain had accepted defeat, in classical fashion, after the fall of Paris, and had tried to adjust to the new situation. The forces led by General de Gaulle built up a continuing unorthodox resistance, without regard to the immediate chances of success.

In similar fashion the Soviet Union failed to impose a communist regime in Finland after it had conquered it militarily in the winter war of 1939-1940.

The government of the United Arab Republic did not collapse when its army and air force were beaten and destroyed by Israel in 1967. Israel could not venture a thrust against Cairo, in spite of the fact that the road lay open before its army. The UAR got a respite to rebuild its forces and resume its aggressive and threatening attitude where it had left them before the war.

The overthrow of the government of Czechoslovakia in 1968 did not come immediately following the armed intervention by the Soviet Union, because it was supported in its course towards liberalization by the overwhelming majority of the people, but only gradually, under continued pressure, and not in the shape of a collapse, but rather as a fading away.

All these are indications of how doubtful the outcome of military action has become today. Another example shows how difficult it has become to take action at all. No nation of the world nor group of nations, and no international organization dared to intervene in order to stop the cruel civil war in Nigeria. It has been of such horror that it dwarfs the horrors commited against Christians in the Ottoman empire which, a century ago, mobilized world opinion and the great powers and led to prompt interventions. We had to look on, powerless, and try to reduce the suffering and the damage done by the ineffectual instrument of humanitarian aid.

The reason for the difficulty of undertaking intervention and for its doubtful effectiveness are to be sought on the one hand within the target society, in the international environment on the other hand.

Modern societies are, whether they are democratically organized or dictatorially ruled, more conscious of their identity. The members are continuously being informed. The information may be true or false, the fact remains that the individual is conscious of being an object of great attention. Hence the individual will be inclined, in case of a national catastrophe, to take himself seriously, take decisions, do something. He or she is less inclined to accept dictation from above, especially when it comes from an antagonist. The individual is, on the grounds of the information previously received, conditioned to identify the aggressor and to oppose him. The knowledge of how to offer resistance, how to fight a clandestine war, and the weapons for it have spread in the course of World War II and of the subsequent conflicts and confrontations, wars of liberation and oppression, all over the world.

Another reason is that material force, including overwhelming armed might, is less feared than in previous times. This is an effect of the spread of technological information. When four score years ago a warship trained its guns on the seaside of a town, people trembled in the expectation of unspeakable horrors and were easily persuaded to surrender. When the steamboat on the Congo river blew its whistle, the Africans were scared into unconditional submission. Today, as a result of the effects of information and propaganda, we are used to thinking only of the atomic bomb as the equivalent of destruction and ultimate horror. Anything less than nuclear annihilation does not seem to impress people any more.

An international environment in which all events are closely linked together, makes any surgical operation directed at one unpleasant spot extremely risky. It has grown difficult or impossible to predict its side effects, its possible amplifications. Whatever the actual military might of a power considering intervention or engaged in intervention may be, it is of doubtful use and of little avail. Restraint is imposed by the danger of expansion and escalation. The outcome is decided more and more not by the amount of power one has, but by the amount of power one can use. So much for the effectiveness of military force.

Similar considerations prevail for economic assistance and military aid when applied as a method for intervening in another nation's affairs. Aid may win a social group which receives it, but fail to reach other important groups, and will antagonize another social group which does not derive any or which thinks that it does not derive enough benefit from it.

Will gifts and sincere efforts to help another nation be rewarded by gratitude? We have learned that this is not the case. Development assistance creates dependence, and dependence is not creative of amity but of dislike and hatred. What are the sociological and political effects of economic assistance? It is impossible to predict it with any accuracy. As we by now have learned in twenty years of almost unbroken social progress in most countries of the world, improved living conditions will not lull people into quiet satisfaction, but rather awake their desire for more and encourage rather than subdue their revolutionary spirit.

There is little reason to believe that military logistic assistance and help in training modern armies will necessarily work for stability. It may, on the contrary, create a new military class, with views different from those held by the constituted government. At the same time, the tools are being provided for the overthrow of this government. Africa gives ample proof for such developments.

The conclusion is that economic help and technological development aid, including one of its special expressions, military assistance, when used as an instrument of intervention, has very uncertain effects. As we have seen, most of the time operations of this type cannot be described as interventions. In the few and special cases where they are actually tools of intervention and used in situations and under conditions which match the definition of intervention, their effect is uncertain and they fail to give full measure of success. Recent experience underlines, as the study of history does, the general futility of intervention of any kind conducted in the spirit of changing a people's way of life and political institutions. Nations generally have the government they deserve.

As we have seen, the triumph of the notion of sovereignty, international public law, public opinion, the international environment and the inadequacy of the instruments of intervention available have made a blunt weapon of intervention. It is less and less likely that powerful nations will be able to restore law and order or what they consider as such in international relations or within an individual state. It is already impossible for the great powers individually to take the law in their own hands. Collective action, even by recognized international bodies and conducted strictly within the limits of their legally recognized powers and procedures, whether conceived as economic and political sanctions or as military sanctions, encounter the same difficulties which beset individual action.

The possibilities to police the world have diminished. Are we therefore bound to drift into a chaotic and anarchic period of history? This need not necessarily be so.

Intervention was conducted, as we have seen, and still is conducted where it survives as an institution of international relations, in the name of a community of thought and of interests, individually or collectively, and with the aim of expanding such a community by imposing its essentials on other nations. Today, by the technological, economic, cultural and human exchange, by the dramatic increase of information made available, which even crosses, in many cases, the artificial barrier set up by the communist regimes against foreign influence, the human community of thought and of interests is growing. We still are far from "One World." But the rivalries, convulsions, conflicts, revolutions, confrontations which we are witnessing and which may be companions of the next generations as well, all stand under the sign of universality. Under this sign the political, philosophical and moral justification for intervention evaporates. It cannot operate between equals. It is not needed. It is not safe. It is not right.

Massive intervention has occurred recently and profoundly altered the course of development which a highly civilized and culturally advanced nation had set for herself—Czechoslovakia.

A massive intervention which has taken the form of a great war has held large parts of Asia under its spell—Vietnam.

The real results of either operation will only gradually emerge when their history and the history of the subsequent years can be written. The uncertainty as to what has been achieved is as great for the authors and planners and decision-makers of the intervention as for the onlooking world. The conclusion to be drawn from these two special events, therefore, corroborates the results of the political, juridical and strategic discussion of interventions past and present: Intervention will have to dissappear from the international scene. Even international actions will be limited to the formal task of keeping international peace, and will fail to influence materially the outcome of a conflict. Other forces will have to solve it.

Index

217